THE SUBJECT OF DEATH AND DYING CAN WE SURVIVE THE DEATH OF A LOVED ONE WITH GRACE?

PRAYING FOR GOD BOOKS: PAT MURRY

authorHOUSE®

AuthorHouse™
1663 Liberty Drive
Bloomington, IN 47403
www.authorhouse.com
Phone: 1 (800) 839-8640

Published by AuthorHouse: 06/06/2016

ISBN: 978-1-5246-1174-3 (sc)
ISBN: 978-1-5246-1173-6 (e)

Print information available on the last page.

Any people depicted in stock imagery provided by Thinkstock are models,
and such images are being used for illustrative purposes only.
Certain stock imagery © Thinkstock.

This book is printed on acid-free paper.

Because of the dynamic nature of the Internet, any web addresses or links contained in this book may have changed
since publication and may no longer be valid. The views expressed in this work are solely those of the author and do
not necessarily reflect the views of the publisher, and the publisher hereby disclaims any responsibility for them.

Scripture quotations marked KJV are from the Holy Bible, King James Version (Authorized Version). First published
in 1611. Quoted from the KJV Classic Reference Bible, Copyright © 1983 by The Zondervan Corporation.

The subject of Death and Dying

Can we survive the death of a loved one with grace?

1st. Thessalonians 4:13-18 (KJV)

Comfort one another with these words.

This is a Biblical interactive work book on the subject of death and dying

CONTENTS

DEDICATION

This book is dedicated to the general public in a sincere effort to help those who wish to become prepared for this eventual day: and to the Pastors that would need to counsel their members, because in their hearts they are overwhelmed by such a great lost.

This book is designed to give each person an opportunity to interact in their own words, negatively or positively concerning their past, or present experiences.

Prayerfully this book will help many people to understand the death process better with less suffering and grief. However we know that many won't be able to cope with the thought of discussing the subject of death, nor the tone of this book, because with some: discussing the subject of death is still taboo even though it is promised to everyone.

If this book can cause one person to get through this process without over extending themselves through the emotion of putting the person away, I have greatly succeeded.

Look at the celebrities who have died lately, and notice how much attention they received after their deaths: this is what we do when one of our loved ones pass, we focus more on them in spending, than we do on how we are going to financially get through the next month, and may I say: And while we are caught up in our emotions, being overwhelmed, and this being the last time to express our love toward this person: we easily overspend.

Let us look at some thoughts and examples on the subject of death and dying.

Please hear my heart on this subject, and know that it is my desire to help and heal suffering souls, this book is not to infuriate anyone. In Jesus name

Let the healing begin.

A WORD ABOUT THE AUTHOR

The author is a student in the school of theology in search of the full knowledge of God, and her doctorate degree. This modern day society has caused us as Christians to search all of the scriptures for the real truth of God. She is the author of the book "when the saints aren't saved" The Spirit of God commands her to write these books in a more simplified form, for better understanding to those who read these books, and maybe like her is not as educated as many others are.

One of her pet peeves is that every male in her house must learn to read, and learn to read well, because knowledge is power.

Pat is the parent of six adult children, five adoptive grandchildren, Seventeen grandchildren and eleven great grandchildren, with two more soon to be born. She has been married fifty three years to one husband.

She is an ordained Minister who practice real estate as a managing broker, she volunteered eight years at Second Helpings, and five years at Lockfield village.

Her hobbies are reading, fishing and travel.

INTRODUCTION

The neglected word of God which Pastors must teach.

This book which I write is very personal to me and the words which are written comes from a deep place of discovery within me. I found in my discovery that we as Christians are called to live the pages of the scriptures; and if we don't or can't follow the path that the scriptures have set for us: then we as Christians have fallen short in life, simply because we are called to this suffering, persecutions, and perfection. We are used by God as examples to others in this life, even in the midst of death and dying.

Why did I write this book on the subject of death and dying?

I wrote this book to help keep us from having to go through such a grieving process; instead of someone having to try and bring us through or out of the grieving process. It is written to help minimize the grieving process. Do you think that this is possible?

Also to me this was the best subject there is, and it is my desire that more people might begin to study the bible on this painful subject of death and dying: as preparation for the next phase of life.

I also chose to write this book on the subject of death and dying, because it is one of the toughest, most urgent, sensitive and neglected subjects in today's society especially in our churches.

The members of our congregations suffer greatly in the areas of; divorce, absentee parents, drug addiction, police brutality and child abuse, but even more so in the area of death and dying than all these other areas of life because of a lack of biblical teaching, wisdom and understanding on our part.

In retrospect we as leaders in times past have not been instructed in the wisdom, and understanding of how we are to respond, and conduct ourselves in these sorrowful times by the word and the will of God. All scriptures are taken from the King James Version of the Bible.

Let us pray

My prayer is, that I am able to effectively articulate to the body of Christ; the need for some strong persuasive teaching according to the word of God on this serious and devastating subject of death and dying.

Let us act on this subject expeditiously as one man and with one voice, by the Holy Spirit. Amen?

Questions to consider:

Do you suppose that this is a worthwhile subject for bible study, or Sunday school class?

Yes. Your comment

No. your comment

If so, how likely are you to participate in these classes, and discussions?

Would you bring a relative: saved or unsaved to this type of class?

What do you suppose the benefits of these classes would be?

What would be the negative side of these classes in your opinion if any?

Discuss at length: write a brief summary on the questions providing your answers in your summary.

Summary and notes:

CHAPTER I

Death and Dying

Let us bring to mind the issue that society is caused to deal with daily, yet somehow we seem to continue to ignore the subject: but now with so much violence and murder in our society and death in our streets daily; we can no longer escape the reality that death has found fertile ground in our cities, towns and country to torment us.

First allow us to determine what do we mean when we speak of death and dying; what approach must we take on this subject? In the old times if our children disagreed with us in what we believe concerning lifestyles: we may become disappointed and disown that child and may even say that he or she is put out of the family; and that he or she is considered dead in our eyes, or one may not believe in Jesus, even the scriptures would call him or her dead.

For an example

"And another of His disciples saith unto Him, Lord, suffer me first to go and bury my father, but Jesus said unto him, follow me; and let the dead bury the dead."

Matthew 8:21, 22 (KJV)

We know that his father wasn't physically dead yet, but he possessed no spiritual life.

Luke speaks on the prodigal son's wayward living. *"For this my son was dead, and is alive again; he was lost, and is found"… Luke 15:24 (KJV)*

We are not speaking of the spiritual death as when we are living outside of the will of God as was the prodigal son, and as the one that wanted to bury his father, but on this subject we are speaking of the natural process of death and dying.

The meaning is when one's breath is gone from the body, which is when the spirit is separated from the body.

As it is written in the book of James which said: *"that for the body without the spirit Or breath, is dead." James 2:26 (KJV)*

This physical separation from the body will surely touch all of us personally at some point in life; so this is my call to all Pastors, Preachers, and teachers, both secular and religious leaders.

This study is written first as a Pastoral care letter; then to the general public.

I would write my thoughts on the preparation of **death and dying**, and our approach is to discover what the word of God has to say to us concerning **death and dying.**

Meaning: life being departed from the body.

There are several things which we must consider.

Who are we speaking about in the course of death and dying?

We are speaking about all people that have breath in this life, for we have been promised by the scriptures that: *"man is appointed once to die then the judgement." Hebrews 9:27 (KJV)*

In all of this we are far from being prepared, even in our salvation and peace with God.

How do we obtain peace with God?

_____

Write four scriptures on peace and salvation

1. _____

2. _____

3. _____

4. _____

Are we warned about our death before it occurs? Yes, give the scripture.

Hint: Deuteronomy 31, 32; 2nd Samuel 12: (KJV)

_____

Is there time to set the house in order? Discuss.

Notes_____

_____

_____

How are we to be comforted concerning the death of a loved one?

Hint: 1st Thessalonians 4, 1st Corinthians 15, Revelation 14: 13 (KJV)

Who should provide this comfort to the suffering people, and by what means are we to be successful? These are just a few questions that we might ask ourselves, and we must also consider what our answers should be.

I believe this comfort should already be in place, by understanding the process in which we are to exit this life through the word of God; in order to avoid the devastation of death.

We as leaders see death in the congregation of our churches, also on the streets of our cities with much pain, agony, and with weeping and much devastation; yet we continue on in life as if this is an isolated incident, and it will always happen to someone else.

Now in this fast pace and dangerous society as the scriptures might say, in these last and evil days, at any moment, and suddenly death may come unaware to overtake one of our own and it will surely leave us bewildered, devastated, confounded and swept off our feet as it has happened to so many others, also it will leave us in a state of fear, shock and disbelief with many questions, why? But when it strikes why should we be so unprepared to deal with this side of life?

Complete this scripture in writing.

"There is a time to be born and a time to die." Ecclesiastes 3: (KJV)

Remember, death is also a part of the living process, like the grass and the trees.

If everything must be put away in its season so must we be put away also, but does it have to be so devastating? I must say not.

As saints God has given us provision for all things including death, but we must be given the word of God which is our only perfect tool to cope with the miseries of death and dying.

Why should we be taught about death in advance?

We know teaching in advance periodically on this subject would cause death not to be a foreign word in our vocabulary and in our perception, and that we may not take on guilt concerning another's death. We also must prepare ourselves for this eventful moment. We must be taught positively concerning this matter, so that death doesn't leave us in fear, shock, devastated and confounded.

We must believe that biblical education teaches us the right response to death; it also withholds the spirit of grief which is from the devil. That we may know that death should not be feared, nor thought of as our enemy.

However we must know that death is the other side of life, and so far death has been our only avenue of escape from this present life, and into the paradise of God. Matthew 22:32 1st Thessalonians 4: 13-18 Psalms 116:15 (KJV) "precious in the sight... Revelation 14:13 (KJV) ... Blessed (or happy) are the dead which die... so the dead is living, put away, sleep, at rest and happy.

How do we justify dying?

Hint: Genesis 3:_____

_____

_____

Understanding the principle

This is the Understanding that God gave to me which caused me to practice these principles with the lack of grief; before my stepfather's death, before we knew that he was terminally ill and dying of cancer; the Holy Spirit spoke to me in advance and said: "call your daddy and apologize to him for any and all the things that you have, and may have said or thought wickedly against him concerning the things done in this life." (You see this was preparation for me) when the Spirit spoke to me concerning him. He (God) reminded me of my thoughts and attitude toward my dad in the past. **Seeking forgiveness is key**.

The scriptures said: *"for if ye forgive men their trespasses, your heavenly Father will also forgive you. Matthew 6:14 (KJV)*

I considered myself to have repented yet I felt so sad, and warned at the same time. I had said to my daddy in the past "I forgive you for everything that you ever did to me," but I had not asked him to forgive me for my actions and attitude that I had towards him.

Today the Holy Spirit brought it all together just as it should be when we begin to set our house in order. So my being older and wiser by the word of the Lord I obeyed the Spirit, and called him and spoke with him, and I apologized to him with a sincere heart concerning what the Spirit had spoken unto me. The spirit was really heavy on me to obey Him with urgency, but daddy said that I had not done him any harm. What I didn't know to say to him was that: "I am so sorry, please forgive me if I have caused you to think, and feel the way you did towards me." I learned this type of repentance through the Spirit of wisdom and by the revelation of God. When I spoke with my father I heard in his voice the sound of weariness, feebleness of life and death. I heard the voice of one subdued, and of someone who was tired of the race and ready to retire.

After our conversation I called my mother and informed her that he wouldn't be with us very long. Two months later I received a phone call from one of his other daughters who was in her fifties; who had never in all of her days called me for any reason, and the message said "call the hospital for he (daddy) had been taken there in serious condition." When I spoke to him he said that the doctors gave him three to six months to live, but three weeks later he was dead. You see, after that I had no need of a funeral nor tears, because the warning and preparation by the Holy Spirit had already been applied unto my heart. And he (my daddy) was already put away in my heart because of that **warning** by the Holy Spirit. God is awesome to me!

Who should you ask for forgiveness, or whom should you release from your spirit through forgiveness? You may privately want to name a few names in prayer.

In your mind would you credit the Holy Spirit with my response to this quietness?

Yes

No

Other _____

Before death calls

When death knocks on our door what is our normal response except; shock, fear, grief, sorrow, devastation, bewilderment and blame.

This should not be the norm, but this will continue to be our natural response until we have learned in advance how to apply the word of God to our hearts on this serious, and devastating subject concerning death and dying.

We know that after so great a time without any teaching on this subject that there may be much resistance, and many of our members may not respond favorably to this teaching. It may very well be because many of them have already had this terrible experience, and some may still have open wounds, and might think that they really can't cope with this torment by reopening the subject. This teaching may very well be the best tool to cause some to be healed.

Ministers are supposed to follow Jesus leading in binding up the brokenhearted.

Hint: Isaiah 61, Ezekiel 34 (KJV)

Have you prepared yourself for that eventful day? If so, how have you prepared yourself?

Write your thoughts here.

_____

_____

_____

_____

Children's response to death is truly the example that we should follow. Yet, we must gently incorporate this teaching into our weekly Bible studies, and monthly sermons **by our church leaders; how long you ask?** Until this word is believed and received into the hearts of the body of Christ. I am certain without a doubt that we **must** quickly integrate this subject into our regular bible studies with scripture, and reference scriptures, experiences and examples, and we as leaders should also become transparent with our members concerning our own responses concerning our own personal, and painful experiences: Allowing them to know that we are learning to cope as well as they, because of what we were or weren't taught on this subject. Transparency is the order of the day we must do this lovingly, and tactfully so not to offend or to seem heartless and insensitive about the matter, but we **must** do this for the sake of our suffering members, as well as for our other members which may not have experienced this type of heartfelt hurt as yet, and so that we don't continue on in this long process of recovery.

If we would teach our congregations these lessons or principles before the fact, there wouldn't be much need for counseling after the fact. These teachings should cause many bereaved family members to understand their feelings, and it should cause them to be healed from their hurt quickly. I believe this would be excellent therapy for all concerned.

As we continue in our argument on this subject of death and dying: I pray that you will earnestly move forward with me as we look into the scriptures for our answers to the relief of death and dying.

Who should teach us on this subject of death and dying?

I would think the people who will have to counsel the bereaved, perform the funerals, and bring words of comfort, they would be the most logical candidates for this job.

Romans 10:14 (KJV) ask the question *"How then shall they hear without a preacher?"*

Yet we have not heard, and these are the very people who have neglected their duties in this area, and caused many people in most cases to be so vulnerable when that eventful day arrives.

Again, I say we as spiritual leaders have greatly errored in the past, but no longer must we continue on in this negligent fashion: we are no longer living in the dark ages where no one speaks of death and dying, even though all must suffer the pain.

Naturally society would lay this error solely at the minister's feet, but we all as a people should take part in this ministry as we grow in this wisdom to comfort.

"Comfort one another with these words" 1ˢᵗ *Thessalonians 4:18 (KJV)* Job 14, 1ˢᵗ Corinthians 15, Revelation 14 (KJV)

However, if we as ministers do not understand the process ourselves, and do not saturate ourselves in the word of God concerning this part of life, how can we as leaders comfort and encourage others?

CHAPTER II

Referring to scriptures for comfort

"For whatsoever things were written aforetime were written for our learning, that we through patience and comfort of the scriptures might have hope." Romans 15:4 (KJV)

Maybe we should first have several conferences around the country on this subject; just for Pastors and other church leaders that we all might become fully equipped in the scriptures, with the same words; without denominational teaching so we all can teach, and learn in the ways of God concerning **death and dying**: and that we may become apt to teach more proficiently on this subject before we bring this teachings to the congregation.

One side of this teaching that we should avoid at all times is encouraging one to embrace that spirit of mourning with our words; you know the words many of us use; "I know that you have been together for forty years and that you are really going to miss this person; some say that they understand and that it's ok to grieve; some say soft words: offer their sympathy then walk away without leaving words of comfort with that bereaved soul.

Our words should be seasoned and full of grace, such as; **"blessed (happy) are the dead that died in the Lord.** *Revelation 14:13 (KJV)* God's way is perfect. I am not saying that all comforting words should be the same as a script, but I am saying that we should be able to bring healing to someone that is searching for peace in their heart. Words which say: "this is right because whatever way a person dies it was Gods' breath; and that life and death is Gods business and not ours.

What one great purpose was there for Moses being in this life? **Search the scriptures.**

_____

_____

Did you know that everyone has only one great purpose for being present in this life? Put the scripture with the person and their purpose for this life.

Sarah _____

Hint: Genesis 21

Judas Iscariot_____

Pharaoh_____

Jesus_____

_____

What is your one and only great purpose for being present in this life?

_____

_____

_____

We must cause people to understand that the assignment in that particular person's life is complete, and there is no other place for that person to go, except back to the Father from which they came, according to Ecclesiastes. 12:7 (KJV)

Moses was our example of this, so we all must at some point return back to the one that sent us. Moses wasn't sick, weak or old per se, but his journey was complete: because God had said to him that he would not be able to enter into the promised land, because of the sin he had committed against Him at the waters of Meribah, so there was no other place for Moses to go, he couldn't go back through the Red Sea into Egypt, nor could he enter into the land of promise, Canaan. So Moses had to return back to the Father in death. Ecclesiastes 12:7

What must we teach others concerning death?

The scriptures tells us that we are to comfort one another with the words which are taken from 1st Thessalonians 4:13-18 (KJV) Even though these words should bring us to worship; how can we ask a person to seriously receive these words of comfort, or even begin to consider worship when they have not been instructed in this word before this eventful act occurs?

At this point these words must sound very hypocritical on our part being done after the fact; like idle words and a perfect way out for us. So we as leaders must teach our members what thus saith the Lord concerning **death and dying** as much as possible, as soon as possible and beforehand; by using the examples from the bible such as Abraham; David and his son by Bathsheba, and Aaron and his sons, Sarah, Jacob, Moses, Job, also our modern day teachers such as John, Robert and Martin. By using these modern day leaders which died; this should cause people to know that the old way of dealing with death in a timely fashion is still the way that we should deal with death today.

I perceive some of you saying: "no one actually does this, this is something that you read about in the Bible; everyone mourns for the loss of a loved one." Yes, you are absolutely correct and that is simply my point, because no one has instructed us nor demonstrated to us anything different.

In most cases members follow their leaders and we as leaders have only demonstrated to others what we have been taught, and that is to mourn and grieve greatly over the dead.

This is not God's way.

The response of David

David was a man after God's own heart according to the scriptures.

"And when He had removed him, (speaking about Saul) He raised up unto them David to be their king; to whom also He gave testimony, and said, I have found David the son of Jesse, a man after mine own heart, which shall fulfill all my will." Acts 13:22 (KJV)

Yet David did not escape the suffering, and the pain of death and dying when it came to his house.

First, let us see what happened with David's dying and dead son: Now, while David's son was <u>dying</u> David was doing all that he could do that his son might live, according to the scriptures.

This is where we are to labour in prayer, fasting and supplicating while one lingers between life and death

2nd Samuel 12:13-24 (KJV) gave to us some excellent insight into how we ought to respond to dying. It said: David wept, fasted and prayed for his sick child **for as long as he lived**, but, when the boy died David rose up, and bathed, sat down and ate bread with no mourning. If we would look just a bit closer we would find that it was not a shock to David that his son died, because in 2nd Samuel 12:14 he was warned that the child would surely die, **just as the saints are warned before their death.**

This is just one more thing that we too often overlook; God never allows these eventful things to come upon the saints without warning.

David was warned of impending death for the child, as was Moses for his brother Aaron and for himself also. Jesus knew His time. This is the goodness of God even under these horrific circumstances.

Let us praise God for the warning of death before it occurs.

Aaron knew that he was to be stripped. President John F Kennedy was warned by the psychic Bette Jean not to go to Dallas because his life was in danger. Robert Kennedy, Joshua and Martin L. King were all warned of their impending deaths, but to our loved ones it will always come as a shock to them unless we begin to teach our people how to cope with death as a natural process. So whenever death may occur it will be well with our souls: not in rejoicing, but without the devastation it brings.

We must learn how to diminish our people's pain and suffering by the word of God.

We must put into effect the action to bind up their wounds, and to heal their broken hearts; just like Jesus did in Isaiah 61: 1,2 and Luke 4:18 (KJV)

2nd Samuel 12:19, 20 (KJV) "David asked his servant's is the child dead? And they said, he is dead."

The scriptures said: "*Then David rose from the earth, and washed, and anointed himself, and changed his apparel,* (he first made himself presentable) then he *went into the house of the Lord and worshiped; then he came to his own house and when he required they set bread before him, and he did eat. And then said his servants onto him, what thing is this that thou hast done? Thou didst fast and weep for the child, while it was alive, but when the child was dead. Thou didst rise and eat bread."*

This is exactly what we should be able to do when death occurs in our families.

The servants were merely servants, and not of the spiritual family and didn't understand the perfect ways of the Godly.

This could have been the perfect time for David to accuse God because of the child's death; which could have caused him to mourn greatly and to sin with his mouth but, because he **had been warned and knew what to expect**; and because he knew it, that made it more tolerable with him.

This is why David was more willingly ready to move on; because he had that time of **preparation in him** (that many of us are cheated of) and he had that time to accept that which had been spoken to him by the prophet Nathan. It reads like this: "*Howbeit, because by this deed thou have given great occasion to the enemies of the Lord to blaspheme, the child also that is born unto thee shall surely die... And the Lord struck the child that Uriah's wife bare unto David, and it was* **very sick.**

Here we see the struggle of death and dying; as we may encounter in any lingering suffering illness, which should cause us to be prepared for this expected death.

Discussion period

How does these fact fit into your life?

_____

_____

Do you think God was too harsh toward the child?

_____

_____

If yes, in your own words give a reasonable response to the question.

_____

_____

If no, explain your answer.

_____

_____

David therefore besought God for the child; and David fasted, and went in, and lay all night upon the earth. And the elders of his house arose, and went to him, to raise him up from the earth; but he would not, neither did he eat bread with them.

And it came to pass on the seventh day that the child died. And the servants of David feared to tell him that the child was dead: For they said, behold while the child was yet alive, we spake unto him, and he would not hearken unto our voice: how will he then vex himself, if we tell him that the child is dead? But when David saw that his servants whispered David perceived that the child was dead: therefore David said unto his servants, is the child dead? And they said; he is dead.

Then David arose from the earth, washed and anointed himself, and changed his apparel, and came into the house of the Lord, and worshipped: then he came to his own house: and when he required, they set bread before him, and he did eat. Then said his servants unto him, what thing is this that thou hast done? Thou didst fast and weep for the child, while it was alive: but when the child was dead, thou didst rise and eat bread. And he said, while the child was yet alive, I fasted and wept; for I said, who can tell whether God will be gracious to me, that the child may live? (Remember David had been warned that the child would surely die.) *But now he is dead, wherefore should I fast? Can I bring him back again?"*

This is the example that we should follow, and not continue on in our mourning, **accept for a brief period of time)** *"David said I shall go to him, but he shall not return to me."*

This is what I am trying so desperately to convey to the people through this reading is that, we must be instructed in the knowledge of God's ways <u>that we may be able to recover quickly and move on in life without the weight of guilt and grief</u>. **The bible went on to say:**

"And <u>David comforted Bathsheba his wife, and went in unto her, and lay with her; and she bare a son, and he called his name Solomon; and the Lord loved him."</u> 2ⁿᵈ Samuel 12:14- 24 (KJV)

Here we see in the comfort of each other; and the understanding of the cause: they both moved back into life quickly, not just one of them moved back into living while the other one yet grieved; but the both of them moved back into life responding to each other in the intimacy of marriage, or relationship. So, that Spirit of mourning which we see every Memorial Day had no opportunity to dominate their lives.

Please, I can't stress this point strong enough, I am not implying nor am I suggesting to anyone not to weep, but I do encourage everyone of us to let every day that passes by be a step closer to truly putting our loved ones to rest in our hearts, and to put them away quickly: so when we visit their graves, should we visit, we don't let that immediate shock of death revive and draw us back into mourning afresh.

The devastation of death and dying

Search the scripture

We as people are devastated when anyone that's near and dear to us passes away suddenly; typically we are not equipped (prepared) in the matters of death and dying as we are taught to prepare for other situations, such as retirement, graduations, college, marriage, and family planning. Neither do we understand that we are here for a season and a greater purpose not only as a family unit, but as sons of God; for fellowship with the Father and to give Him praise. We are here for only one great purpose in our lives, and we have great examples of this in the Bible; such as Sarah, she lived eighty nine years in the mist of ridicule and persecution because she was barren, but in the ninetieth year of her life she brought forth **her one and only great purpose** for her being in this world; **which was that seed of promise which was Isaac.**

*"And God said, Sarah thy wife shall bear thee a son indeed: and thou shall call his name Isaac: and I will establish my covenant with him for an everlasting covenant and with his seed after him. But my covenant will I establish with Isaac, **which Sarah shall bear unto thee at this set time next year." Genesis 17:19-21 (KJV)***

*"And the Lord visited Sarah as He had said, and the Lord did unto Sarah as He had spoken for Sarah conceived, and bare Abraham a son in his old age, at the **set time** of which God had spoken to him. And Abraham called the name of his son that was born unto him, **whom Sarah bare to him,** Isaac." Genesis 21: 1-3 (KJV)*

After her purpose was accomplished not much was spoken about Sarah accept to say, Sarah died. Genesis 23: 1-20 (KJV) Verse 1 gives us her age at her death, also where she died, then

Verse 2 speaks of Abraham's mourning as if it was brief, then it moves on to speak about a burying place for her. After that in Verse 19 the scriptures said "*and after that, Abraham buried Sarah his wife in the cave of the field of Machpelah before Mamre: the same is Hebron in the land of Canaan.*

With no mentioning of any <u>great</u> mourning only a little mourning from Abraham. Where is Isaac and the family? I am sure they were there, but the point is to show how quietly she was put away, then a search for a burying place, after that she was buried.

In the book of Genesis 24:67 we find that Isaac takes a wife and is comforted by his wife after his mother's death. No more is mentioned of Sarah's death. In other words he moved on with his life.

Question:

Do you realize had Abraham met his second wife Keturah on the way back from the burying ground of his former wife Sarah, and had he decided to marry Keturah on their way back from the cemetery it would have been perfectly alright and in order?

What did you say! After all the marriage contract said: **until death do us part** the contract has been satisfied. Remember, Sarah is dead and the marriage covenant has been fulfilled. But man has much tradition and in his tradition this causes a couple to remain separated for a year or more because we say it's improper and we do frown on such action; but this is proper to do because of the fulfillment of the covenant agreement.

Although some family members would think hard of the one that remarried so Soon: because man's culture and customs have said that we need that lengthy mourning period: but this is not scriptural.

Somehow we forget that in most cases of long illnesses the intimacy of the marriage has already been lost to pain, medicine and bed pans, the couple remained together as part of their marriage covenant and out of love for each other, but the intimacy of that union in most cases died long ago.

Discuss why one should or should not wait a year or so to remarry if they so choose, consider circumstances such as maybe that person is sick also, and needs a companion or maybe they are ready for some intimacy without sinning.

Discuss and take notes for judgement sake.

Our examples

If we were to search the scriptures we would find many of the examples which God used. Sarah was just one example, we also have Abraham, Jacob, Joseph's father, Moses in his "death and perfect dying", Aaron, and Aaron's sons, these are just a few people who we saw die in the scriptures, and the type and ***time frame for mourning that was prescribed to the people of God; by God Himself.*** **Maybe because we don't point out this time frame for mourning, people can't accept a brief process of mourning; it causes them to feel guilty if they feel happy too soon simply because of Mans' tradition. Now, do we suppose that our ways are wiser than God's ways?**

Is His ways more perfect than ours? If so, when do we begin to practice what the word of God is saying to us? Now, if we can look beyond our own hurt because our loved one is departed: we might realize that we are to rejoice in their death; and to celebrate their death as life lived.

Psalms 116:15 (KJV) tells us, *precious in the sight of the Lord is the death of His saints.*

(And I heard a voice from heaven saying unto me, write, blessed (happy) are the dead which die in the Lord from henceforth; yea, saith the Spirit that they may rest from their labours and their works do follow them) Revelation 14:13 (KJV)

Why do we grieve?

First, we are already set in the heart of God for purpose, then we must be born into the world and into the right family, we grow up; live, love, fulfill our purpose in life then we must pass-on (die.) But this really is where we must ask ourselves that great question, why do we grieve? Could it be because they miss us so much, I can't fathom that or do we miss them instead, or are we sad because they have escaped this life, and left us here alone to continue on this rugged road of life without them?

Are they sad to have escaped the sufferings of this life? Not if they are saved for they have been blessed to return back to the presence, and paradise of the Lord.

Then shall the dust return to the earth as it was; and the spirit shall return unto God who gave it. Ecclesiastes 12:7 (KJV)

I believe if we would consider the situation we would find that our grief, sorrow and pain is mainly about us, and not so much about the dead, but it is about how we are going to be able to continue on in this life without the presence of that person.

Personal transparency:

When I found myself in this possible situation of the death of my husband, my first thoughts were about me being left alone in this big house, next was the thought of downsizing in-order to make ends meet, after that was the thought on how to convince my young sons that it was alright, next was the thought of losing his income; in other-words everything was about how we which were left behind was going to fair, but in too many cases we carry some type of guilt, and some times there are circumstances surrounding a person's death that pierce our hearts through more than the actual death. Our minds continue to remember the tragedy of their death, which causes us great pain whether it be a violent death or sudden death, an automobile accident, or whether it be a missing person found dead, a kidnapping and rape murder, or suicide.

It is sometimes the circumstances which we associate with their death which causes this thing to consumes us, sometimes we feel that we could have done more on their behalf, or we should have been more tolerant or done a better job in their lives while they yet lived, and now we have missed the opportunity to make things right.

Too many times we remember their last words, and maybe we didn't honor their last request not knowing that this would be the last time to do such, or we didn't have an opportunity to say goodbye. Many times we were recently in their presence and didn't realize that this would be the last time; maybe our last words were harsh and bitter toward them. (This is the spirit of guilt that adds to the enemy's binding power against us, **let it go.**) If we would be honest with ourselves we would realize that it is our own pain that causes us to grieve as we do.

Can we hear this? Is it mainly about us and what we consider our loss? Either way the spirit of grief finds its place with us, and it will surely keep us bound in the graveyard much too long while life with the living pass us by. Of course this spirit of guilt and bondage is from the enemy, God would have us to be free.

Question:

Can you release your loved one into their proper perspective, and begin to laugh and love again? You are not being unfaithful to them when you begin to have fun, and enjoy life again remembering them less: this process is to cause them to no longer remain in the forefront of life, but they must at some point move into that safe and quiet place of your heart, not to be forgotten, but causing them to rest, and give to you that perfect memory of them without torment and guilt.

Question:

What was the reaction of death too the people of old?

Let us begin our journey with Abraham. Genesis 25 speaks on the death of Abraham, and it said less about his death than some others that maybe wasn't considered to be as great as Abraham was.

"And these are the days of the years of Abraham's life which he lived, an hundred threescore and fifteen years.

Then Abraham gave up the ghost, and died in a good old age, an old man, and full of years; and was gathered to his people". Genesis 25:7, 8 (KJV)

Here again, we see no great mourning concerning the death of Abraham; then the scriptures move on to the next step, let us not forget that Genesis 25: 1, 2 (KJV) tells us that Abraham took a wife and her name was Keturah.

In verse 2. We find that Abraham had other sons by his second wife Keturah, we also noticed in verse 9, that <u>Isaac and Ishmael</u> are the <u>only one's mentioned in the time of his burial.</u>

Verse 9. And his sons Isaac and Ishmael buried him in the cave of Machpelah, in the field of Ephron the son of Zohar the Hittite, which is before Mamre

These scriptures show to us the peace and quiet of their burials and the response of their children, friends and relatives.

It is the examples of the scriptures that should speak to our hearts in times of death and dying and **not our emotions**, and this will work well if we are preconditioned in the word of God, but until we are rooted and grounded in the word of God this spirit of grief will continue to overtake and plunder us. Let the men and women of God hear, understand and teach to the congregations the lessons on death and dying according to the scriptures.

Question:

How do you feel about the things you have read, and how would you have dealt with these situations had this been you?

_____

_____

Do you have a greater perspective on this subject? If so, explain and discuss.

CHAPTER III

Continuing the process
Next we have Jacob, Joseph's father.
Geneses 50: 1-14 (KJV)

And Joseph fell upon his father's face, and wept upon him, and kissed him."

The book said he wept on him, it is good to weep; but we are to refrain from grief and that sorrowful spirit of mourning.

"And Joseph commanded his servants the physicians to embalm his father; and the physicians embalmed Israel". And forty days" were fulfilled for him; for so are fulfilled the days of those which are embalmed; (it took forty days to embalm him not forty days of mourning for the family, but threescore days for the Egyptians) *"and the Egyptians mourned for him Threescore and ten days".*

Verse 4-A" and when the days of his mourning were past...

Yet, 10 said: *"and they came to the threshing floor of Atad, which is beyond Jordan, and there they mourned with a great and very sore lamentation;* **and he made mourning for his father seven days".**

If we were to look a bit closer we would find that *when the inhabitants of the land, the Canaanites, saw the mourning in the floor of Atad they said,* (this is a **grievous mourning to the Egyptians;** *wherefore the name of it was called Abel-mizraim, which is beyond Jordan."*

"And Joseph returned into Egypt, he, and his brethren, and all that went up with him to bury his father, after he had buried his father".

Question

If Jacob had been your father who had died; could anyone have said to you leave the children at home while we go up? Wow! Don't this sound harsh, only let us hear and see what happened in the scriptures. I know **most** of us won't even consider this action.

Observe this, in verse 8 the scriptures said "that their little ones were left at home... You see we think that this is an outrage because we have been conditioned to think that this is the last time that the children will see mama, grandpa or grandma; so we continue to do things according to mans tradition, and not according to the word of the Lord.

It is not Gods' way nor His will that we should suffer hard and long as we do, and as we have done in the past. In Mark's gospel Jesus made a statement that we sometimes don't quiet grasp *"do ye not therefore err, because ye know not the scripture, neither the power of God?"* Mark 12:24 (KJV)

Here we understand that he is speaking to the Sadducees, but to those that would dispute what I am saying, the same principles apply to us concerning death and dying for in this matter we do not know the scriptures, neither do we know God's power to heal us.

Then he went on to say: Verse 26 *"And as touching the dead, that they rise; have ye not read in the book of Moses, how in the bush God spake unto him, saying, I am the God of Abraham, and the God of Isaac, and the God of Jacob?"*

Remember; to us these men are dead, But God said in *Verse 27 "that He is not the God of the dead but the God of the living. Ye therefore do greatly err"*. God said that they are alive; He said that He is their God. To God they are put away, to us they are dead. That alone tells us that our thinking is not in line with God's thinking concerning death and dying, because we have not learned the scriptures neither can we put them into practice.

Not permitted to mourn as others

Why should we mourn?

Here, we are speaking of the two sons of Aaron which offered strange fire unto the Lord, and died. Aaron, because he wore the priestly garments was not permitted to mourn for his sons as others, or as they would do with the hair hanging loose, tearing of the clothes, the head uncovered, ashes on the head, nor the viewing of the body; nor kissing his dead sons goodbye.

Think about this, they were still his sons whether they were right or wrong, yet he had instructions not to move out of his place, or position because of their deaths; this man had to remain on his post and continue on in his office or duties inspite of his personal circumstances.

How often do we shut everything down and rush to the hospital, the family home, or we may rush to console someone when we hear of a death that's close to us?

Hear is another Question for you

If this had been your mother or your father which had died could anyone have said to you don't cry, be still, don't go yet, or let's finish this job then we will go, and if not why not?

Yes

No

Why not?

How do you feel about these questions?

_____

_____

Remember, the act of death is already complete why can't we wait another few minutes, or another hour before we rush to be by our relatives or our friend's side?

My personal answer

Because of shock, fear, disbelief, sorrow and grief, just the mention of the word death completely robs us of our strength, assignment, faith, and our peace; we allow death to completely wreck us.

Death has too much power over us as people of God. But this is what Aaron had to do; he had to remain in his position as a priest, and not be moved out of his position **because** of his son's deaths; he was not allowed to weep for his sons because of his position as high priest.

Let us look at his position in Leviticus

The death of his sons

"And Nadab and Abihu, the sons of Aaron, took either of them his censer and put fire therein, and put incense thereon, and offered strange fire before the Lord, which he commanded them not" And there went out fire from the Lord, and devoured them, and they died before the Lord. Then Moses said unto Aaron, this is it that the Lord Spake, saying, I will be sanctified in them that come nigh me, and before all the people I will be glorified. And Aaron held his peace.

And Moses called Mishael and Elzaphan, the sons of Uzziel the uncle of Aaron, (relatives) and said unto them, come near, carry your brethren from before the sanctuary out of the camp. So they went near, and carried them in their coats out of the Camp; as Moses had said." Leviticus 10:1-7 (KJV)

Remember there was a fire that came out from God yet there were bodies to be buried. Here we are reminded of what Aaron already knew from the word which the Lord gave Moses. Aaron knew the law of the vow of consecration and it goes like this.

Let's look at another chapter of scriptures.

"All the days that he separateth himself unto the Lord he shall come at no dead body".

"He shall not make himself unclean for his father, or for his mother, for his brother, or for his sister, when they <u>die</u>; because the consecration of God is upon his head". Numbers 6: 6, 7 (KJV)

You might say that Aaron had to do that because of his job, you are right but this attitude should apply to everyone, he was our example in the position of our modern day Pastors.

"And he that is the high priest among his brethren, upon whose head the anointing oil was poured, and that is consecrated to put on the garments, shall not uncover his head, nor rend his clothes. Neither shall he go in to any dead body, nor defile himself for his father, nor for his mother, neither shall he go <u>out of the sanctuary</u>, nor profane the sanctuary of his God; for the crown of the anointing oil of his God is upon him; I am the Lord." Leviticus 21:10-12 (KJV)

We understand that this is Old Testament, but the principles are the same we are to carry on with our duties in spite of our present circumstances.

"Whatsoever things were written aforetime was written for our learning that through patience and comfort of the scriptures we might have hope." Romans 15:4 (KJV)

Let us return to the original scriptures.

Verse 6 said "And Moses said unto Aaron, and unto Eleazar and unto Ithamar, his sons" We see here that the brothers are in the same situation as their father Aaron. They also must present a peaceful attitude because of who they are. *"Uncover not your heads, neither rend your clothes; lest you die, and lest wrath come upon all the people; <u>but let your brethren, the whole house of Israel, bewail the burning which the Lord has kindled."</u>*

<u>*And ye shall not go out from the door of the tabernacle of the congregation, lest ye die; for the anointing oil of the Lord is upon you. And they did according to the words of Moses".*</u>

Here we saw that Aaron, the dead boys' father wasn't to carry on as others, even his brothers were to remain in their places while the funeral was in progress.

My! What strength they received when they heard a word from the Lord through Moses. Refer to Leviticus 10:3, 6, 7 (KJV)

It is a glorious thing to me that God has a will for our lives, and that He can cause us to submit to His will without anguish if we are willing.

'Here is another question for you:

Why does a Pastor or Minister carry on as the common man does when his wife, mother, or his favorite son or daughter dies? Has he or she not heard; have we not read what thus saith the

Lord, as it is written according to the scriptures, does not the word of God apply to leadership first as it did to the nation of Israel?

Are we not supposed to be excellent examples of God as to how we are to respond to the issues of life, even such as death and dying?

As leaders are we not to be the first partakers of the word with much wisdom, and in demonstration to others as the Jews were first? If Jews as chosen leaders were first in all things, then we as chosen leaders of the church must be likewise according to the scriptures.

Question:

How do you feel about not having any instructions in this area of life from the church?

_____

_____

Should Pastor do more teaching on this subject in the positive aspect?

_____

_____

Do you consider Pastors to be negligent in this area of Christian living?

_____

_____

Speaking to the Jews first

"Then Paul and Barnabas waxed bold, and said, it was necessary that the word of God should first have been spoken to you; but seeing that you put it from you, and judged yourselves unworthy of everlasting life, lo, we turn to the gentiles" Acts 13:46 (KJV)

*"Tribulation and anguish, upon every soul of man that, **doeth evil of the Jew first**, and also of the gentile; but glory, honour, and peace, to every man that worketh good, **to the Jew first**, and also to the gentile." Romans 2: 6-10 (KJV)*

*"**But shewed first unto them** of Damascus, and at Jerusalem, and throughout all the coast of Judaea, **and then to the gentiles**, that they should repent and turn to God, and do works meet for repentance." Acts 26:20 (KJV)*

If we had any reservations about our positions in life, and how we should be examples to others, I believe our positions are now made very clear by the word of God; we just need to believe it and respond accordingly.

Pastors: are you ready to move forward in this ministry of death and dying?

Yes _____

No_____

Maybe _____

Why not? _____

CHAPTER IV

The departing of Aaron setting the house in order

Then we have Aaron himself in Numbers 20:1-29 (KJV) please read this carefully that you may see not only the warning of death, but the transfer of his office to his son by his brother in the same setting.

Even in our death and dying we must continue to set our house in order, not only our personal affairs but also the house of God, and this is what is happening in this case.

"And the <u>Lord spoke unto Moses and Aaron</u> in Mount Hor, by the coast of the land of Edom saying", Aaron shall be gathered to his people; for he shall not enter into the land which I have given unto the children of Israel, because ye rebelled against my word at the water of Meribah".

We must be careful never to say that the word of God is not enough because we are human. Here God gives to them the warning of death, and the reason why Aaron will not enter into the Promised Land; just as he gave to David the reason why the child would surely die.

"Take Aaron (remember this is Moses brother) again I say, the scripture said: "Take Aaron and Eleazar his son, and bring them up unto Mount Hor"

And strip Aaron of his garments, and put them upon Eleazar his son; and Aaron shall be gathered unto his people, and shall die there".

This is the warning that his brother is about to die before he and his son's eyes, by the action that Moses must take.

Question:

How would you like to have a hand in your loved one's death, and be able to do this without grief or regret?

Life was tough for these people, because they trusted and obeyed the word of God, God made the transition bearable for them as He will also do for us, God is truly capable.

At the end of verse 29 the scripture said: and when the entire congregation saw that Aaron was dead, **they mourned for Aaron thirty days**; even all the house of Israel".

This man had been their high priest for years as some of our Pastors are, yet another Priest had already been chosen, and installed or positioned into his office, even before the death of the first

Priest, and without the congregation's input or their vote, **and they mourned for their former Priest for only thirty days.)**

Question:

Why does it take us so long to replace our Pastors when one of them dies?

My Answer: Because we have not made the proper preparation for this day, by grooming another through much prayer and supplication while this leader yet lives.

In most cases we have to wait too long to find someone of our choice to take his place, in the meanwhile the flock suffers and wanders about looking for stability, and while they are wandering too many of them are caught in a snare of the devil, and many die because they couldn't find their way back to the house of the Lord.

I am a bit frantic about this, this is not the order of things; the scriptures said that we are to know them that labor among us, so why don't we as leaders know who should be the next in line for this duty through God's revelation?

"And we beseech you, brethren, to know them which labour among you, and are over you in the Lord, and admonish you; And to esteem them very highly in love for their work's sake. And be at peace among yourselves." 1ˢᵗ *Thessalonians 5:12, 13 (KJV)*

If the congregation doesn't except that person and some begin to wander and die in their wanderings, then I am sure that their blood would be on their own heads and not ours.

God is not heartless are we being contrary to his order?

Then Moses himself had warning of his death, and like Aaron, **they were commanded to mourn thirty days, then they were to move on.**

If God had not allotted to them a certain time period for weeping or mourning (your choice) they would have remained there in the wilderness so much longer because of Moses death; and I am sure that the majority of them would have remained right there until they died, but God told them to move on into the Promised Land and live.

Our lives must continue on joyfully because the assignment and purpose for our loved ones being in this life has now been fulfilled, whatever that assignment may have been it is done.

Numbers 27: 12, 13 & 14-16 (KJV) *"Now the Lord said unto Moses, "Get thee up into this mount Abarim, and see the land which I have given to the children of Israel.*

And when thou hast seen it, **thou also shall be gathered unto thy people, as Aaron thy brother was gathered".**

Again, He warns him of his impending death; don't you just love the fact that God thinks enough of us to warn us of our death that we might set our house in order?

"For ye rebelled against my commandment in the desert of Zin, in the strife of the congregation, to sanctify me at the water before their eyes; that is the water of Meribah in Kadesh in the wilderness of Zin. Numbers 27:14-16 (KJV)

And Moses spake unto the Lord, saying, let **the Lord, the God of the spirits of all flesh, set a man over the congregation.**

We have much more on these saints concerning their "death and dying."

In Deuteronomy 31:14-A, and 16. In verse 14-A, (KJV) the Scriptures show to us clearly the warning of death and the transfer of duty.

Verse 14-A, this is his warning; "and the Lord said unto Moses, Behold thy day's approach that thou <u>must die.</u>"

Remember that they were at the end of their forty year wilderness journey and like his brother Aaron; Moses could not enter into the Promised Land, after the warning of his death he was instructed to move forward in the transfer of his power to another; as we saw with his brother Aaron, only this transfer of power is to Joshua.

Moses didn't have time to mourn or grieve even for himself, because he had unfinished business with completing the work of God, and in getting his own house in order.

Man! Isn't this awesome?

Verse 14-B (KJV) said, *"Call Joshua, and present yourselves in the tabernacle of the congregation, that I may give him a charge".*

Did you notice in most of our examples that when the word of death was spoken to them, they always went to the house of God to worship?

Then it went on to say *"And Moses and Joshua went, and presented themselves in the tabernacle of the congregation."*

Afterward in Deuteronomy 34: 5-8 we see here that Moses died, we see his obituary that he was buried, how old he was at the time of his death; and the time period prescribed; I repeat, **the time period prescribed by God** of their mourning or weeping. This is how it went.

"So Moses the servant of the Lord died…

This is the main point that we need to try very hard to remember; that when death comes to our family that this person didn't belong to us, but he or she belonged to God, and that person was in service to God and not to us persa. We were only the Stewards which God had given to have the charge over them for a little season until they were grown, or until their assignment was complete, then they would return to Him from which they came. *Ecclesiastes 12:7(KJV)*

Verse 5 "So Moses the servant of the Lord died there in the land of Moab, according to the word of the Lord".

"And He (God that is) buried him in a valley in the land of Moab, over against Beth-peor; but no man knoweth of his sepulcher unto this day".

This is an excellent example of God knowing, that if the people had known where Moses' grave was, the majority of them if not all of them would have remained in that place **(graveyard)** forever, and would have built an altar, and an image and a shrine there and worshiped it, and would have died there because they would have gotten caught up in the spirit of mourning and memory **like so many of us do,** and they would not have moved into the land of promise.

Verse 7 said: "And Moses was an hundred and twenty years old when he died; his eye was not dim, nor his natural force abated".

Verse 8 said: *"And the children of Israel <u>wept for Moses in the plains of Moab thirty days; so the days of weeping and mourning for Moses were ended".</u>*

Minister in discussion on how to prepare and put away love ones, and the difference between the saved and the unsaved, how to handle this type of sorrow.

Write._____

_____

_____

_____

_____

_____

_____

Your personal notes:

Joshua quietly passes on

In the 23rd Chapter of the book of Joshua we see Joshua, the man that finally had peace in his reign going off the scene. It said in the last line that: *"Joshua was old and stricken in age... And Joshua called for all Israel, and for their elders, and for their heads, and for their judges, and for their officers, and said unto them, I am old and stricken in age" Joshua 23:1, 2 (KJV)*

Here we see another great leader making preparation for his death; and he is setting both his house and God's house in order before he dies.

This is a man like Moses who had been with this people for such a long time, he was like a mother and father to them; one who had loved and protected them, and caused them to have favor with God, and one who was chosen by God to lead them. They knew this man who had labored among them for such a long time, and he was accepted by them as God's man to lead them.

In the end of his life he caused the nation to renew the covenant with the Lord. Yet in the end of his life we find him quietly passing off the scene, this is awesome to me!

*"And it came to pass after these things that Joshua the son of Nun, **the servant of the Lord died,** being an hundred and ten years old. And they buried him in the border of his inheritance in Timnathserah, which is in Mount Ephraim, on the north side of the hill of Gaash". Joshua 24:29, 30 (KJV)*

There is no mention whatsoever of any public mourning for the death of this great General, and there wasn't any mention of anyone in particular mourning or weeping over him.

Wow! This is good!

Eleazar

We saw the Priest Eleazar the son of Aaron die, and they buried him in a hill that pertained to Phinehas his son, which was given him in Mount Ephraim. Joshua 24:33 (KJV)

We see again the process of death and dying of the men of old; men who had served God, and the people for a number of years, yet, after their deaths it was as if it was a natural occurrence and all was well.

This is the attitude that we must learn to take when one of our loved ones dies, not only that, but in most cases we ought to openly rejoice; this is the order which is given unto us from the scriptures.

Question

How do you feel about the quietness of the putting away of these great Patriots?

_____

_____

Could you have been so gracious in this putting away?

Yes

No

If not, Why not?

_____

_____

_____

Let us pray:

Heavenly Father, you are wonderful: thank you for the warning of death that we are not only able to set your house in order; but there is time also for us to set our personal house in order. In Jesus name we pray. Amen

CHAPTER V

This is the greatest example

Let us see how Job responds to the death of his children, in many cases death enters into the family suddenly, but normally its one death at a time. We have automobile accidents, strokes, murder, heart attacks, lingering suffering deaths, SID's and many other sudden deaths, and too many times we find ourselves stunned and in a daze from shock, yet we get to see Job's reaction when he got the bad news that all ten of his children were dead at the same time.

Remember, this is the man that it was said of him by God Himself, *that he was perfect and upright, he feared God, and eschewed evil. Job 1:1 (KJV)*

Yet, death visited his house with a vengeance, so we know that death is a fact of life and it does not discriminate.

First it was his oxen and his asses, this is striking his wealth, then his servants, this is striking his laborers, next were the sheep and the servants. Some things we think we can cope with, other things we say "that can be replaced", and then came the tough shocking news that his seven sons and three daughters were dead.

How devastated Job must have been, let us see how Job will handle this grievous situation.

Job 1:1-22 (KJV) please read this in its entirety.

Job 1:18 (KJV) said: *"while he was yet speaking, there came also another, and said, thy sons and thy daughters were eating and drinking wine in their eldest brother's house".*

Isn't that just like the enemy to publish all negative news? Just to let everyone know whether or not you were caught in sin, by murder, drunkenness or drinking, or whether you committed suicide, or accidentally overdosed on drugs, or whether you got caught in an adulterous act. Or if you died violently. If we heard this bad news about our loved ones we would grieve all the more, because we would begin to wonder if they had gone to heaven or Hell. But, If we had known what the word of God had to say about a persons life and living; we would already have the answers to our questions concerning them in their death process whether we wanted to accept the verdict or not.

As I recall Job prayed and made offerings for his children every day in case they had sinned against God, and cursed God in their hearts.

"And his sons went and feasted in their houses, every one his day; and sent and called for their three sisters for to eat and to drink with them."

And it was so, when the days of their feasting were gone about, that Job sent and sanctified them, and rose up early in the morning, and offered burnt offerings according to the number of them all; for Job said, it may be that my sons have sinned, and cursed God in their hearts, Thus Job did continually" Job 1:4, 5 (KJV)

*"And behold, there came a great wind from the wilderness, and smote the four corners of the house, and it fell upon the young men, and they are dead; and I only am escaped to tell thee" Then Job arose, and rent his mantle, and shaved his head, (this was an expression of grief in their day), and fell down upon the ground, **and worshipped".*** Job 1: 19, 20 (KJV)

As David did worship, as **Aaron and Moses went to the house of worship** and must have worshiped there, as we must also learn to worship in these trying times of crisis. **Worship is the order of the day.**

Here we find that **under the worse circumstances that worship is the order of the day**, and not despair frustration and accusations.

"And said, naked came I out of my mother's womb, and naked shall I return thither; the Lord gave, and the Lord hath taken away: blessed be the name of the Lord." Job 1:21, 22 (KJV)

Here we don't see a great and separate mourning for Job's children by any other family members, or friends even though he thought God was doing this to him, we know he must have been in great distress, **yet, he went to God for his comfort while he was in the midst of his distress.**

Job showed to us that in these times of trouble and death that this is really the time to bless the Lord and curse not. (Job understood that these children belonged to God.)

"In all this Job sinned not, nor charged God foolishly.

"So Job died, being old and full of days". Job 42:17 (KJV)

We realize that his death was not the focal point of his story; yet, when he died there was no mention of a great mourning for Job he quietly moved off the scene.

As important as a brief mourning process is, we must not make it the focal point of a person's life, because of the lack of education according to the scripture on the subject of death and dying, we don't quite know how to respond to death and dying with dignity, and how to just let it pass from us. Remember the scriptures said: "My people are destroyed for lack of knowledge"... Hosea 4: 6 (KJV) Again, it is the word of God that makes us wise and stable in all situations.

Question

How do you see your response if you were in Job's shoes, you not knowing his story?

_____

_____

_____

Would you be hostile toward God, and was Job's test too harsh?

_____

_____

_____

Could you have worshipped God so soon in this situation?

_____

_____

Do you think the word of God is your best resource for healing, and would you use it?

Yes

No

Give an explanation for each answer.

_____

_____

_____

Looking at Jesus

Let us find out just who is this Jesus that we dare to speak of; as we take a closer look at the one who came into the world with a greater purpose on His life than all the others that came before Him. We find that He was the perfect man without spot or wrinkle, He was the only one to save the world from sin and this is His resume, *God Himself (called the word) put on flesh and dwelt among us. John 1:14 (KJV)*

This is the same one that so loved the world that He laid down His life for the sheep.

Actually it said; *"as the Father knoweth me, even so know I the Father and I lay down my life for the sheep." St. John 10:15-18 (KJV)*

Verse 18 said *"no man taketh it from me, but I lay it down of myself. I have power to lay it down, and I have power to take it again. This command have I received of my Father."*

"But we see Jesus, who was made a litter lower than the angels for the suffering of death, crowned with glory and honour; that He by the grace of God should taste death for every man." Hebrews 2:9 (KJV)

But when this great man's purpose of teaching, training the Apostles, and ministering to the world the ministry of love one to another, the forgiveness of sin, and bringing forth miracles in their midst: thus it was time for Him to depart for His great purpose in this world or in this life was finished. So the next step was for Him to do what all the other people which came before Him had done, such as Moses and all the prophets, and that was to return to the Father by way of death.

In the 16th chapter of St. John's Gospel; Jesus tells His followers *"A little while, and you shall not see me; and again, a little while, and you shall see me, because I go to the Father".*

"Then said some of His disciples among themselves, what is this that He saith unto us, a little while, and you shall not see me; and again, a little while you shall see me; and, because I go to my Father? They said therefore, what is this that He saith, a little while? We cannot tell what He saith".

"Now Jesus knew that they were desirous to ask Him, and He said unto them, do you enquire among yourselves of that I said, a little while, and you shall not see me; and again, a little while, and you shall see me?" Verily, verily, I say unto you, that you shall weep and lament, but the world shall rejoice; and you shall be sorrowful, **but your sorrow shall be turned into joy***". St. John 16:16-20 (KJV)*

The last line said, *"I go to prepare a place for you... St. John 14:2 (KJV)* As in St. John 20:20 (KJV)

We should be happy as they were, because we know who the Lord Jesus is and that He is a part of us.

In St. John's gospel we notice that after Jesus was crucified, the scriptures make no mention of the disciples making a great mourning for Jesus even though they didn't know the scriptures, that is, in three days *He must rise again from the dead. St John 20:9 (KJV)*

But we saw them in fear for their own lives because of what had happened to Jesus.

For as yet they knew not the scriptures; that He must rise again from the dead".

After they had gone to the sepulcher, and found not the body of Jesus,

"Then the disciples went away again to their own home." St John 20:10 (KJV)

Here we see one mourner over Jesus

"But Mary Magdalene stood without at the sepulcher weeping; and as she wept, she stooped down, and looked into the sepulcher" and seeth two angels in white sitting, the one at the head, and the other sitting at the feet, where the body of Jesus had lain. And they say unto her, woman, why weepest thou? She said unto them, because they have taken away my Lord, and I know not where they have laid Him", John 20:9-13 (KJV)

This is as if He was Lost (this is how we see the dead as being lost.) remember, they are not lost, but they are put away.

If we were to consider weeping because of a great loss; then the world should still be weeping for what we call the death of Jesus, but because we know the story of His death which we gained through the reading of the scriptures; how He purchased salvation for the world and that we have redemption through His blood...

F*or this we celebrate and rejoice in His death* (and mourn not) every year at the season which we call Easter (which is our death, burial and resurrection season) in memory of His crucifixion, and His resurrection we celebrate!

The Passover which the Jews celebrate year by year we all remember, and celebrate the Passover. Then we give praise to God for His resurrected life in the days in that which we call Christmas, this is when we celebrate His birth.

As Isaiah said: *"Unto us a child is born, unto us a son is given; and the government shall be upon His shoulder; and His name shall be called wonderful, counselor, the mighty God, the everlasting Father, the prince of peace." Isaiah 9:6 (KJV)*

Then Matthew said: *"And she shall bring forth a son, and thou shall call His name Jesus; for He shall save His people from their sins". "Now all this was done, that it might be fulfilled which was spoken of the Lord by the Prophet, saying, "Behold a virgin shall be with child and shall bring forth a son, and they shall call His name Emmanuel, which being interrupted is, God with us." Matthew 1:21-23 (KJV)*

We celebrate His death every time we take the communion in remembrance of Him which we are commanded to do. But, we do this without sorrow and grief without weeping and mourning; not as in loss but as in gain through His death we have victory.

The book of 1st Corinthians said: *"for I have received of the Lord that which also I delivered unto you, that the Lord Jesus the same night in which He was betrayed took bread" "And when He had given thanks, He brake it, and said, Take, eat; this is my body, which is broken for you; <u>this do in remembrances of me."</u> 1st Corinthians 11:23-25 (KJV)* <u>this is our memorial unto Him:</u> This is the time and the place that we are to worship Him.

We are to do this unto the Lord in a solemn assembly not as with pain and sorrow, and not as a reminder of a tragic event as we do concerning our deceased loved ones at certain seasons; such as birthdays, a wedding anniversary, the Christmas season, our resurrection week and Memorial Day. But we celebrate His death with joy, praise and gratitude for His sacrifice for our souls. We should remember our loved ones death just as we remember Jesus' death, joyfully as life lived.

"After the same manner also He took the cup, when He had supped, saying, This cup is the New Testament in my blood; <u>this do ye, as oft as ye drink it, in remembrance of me."</u>

This is our call to a celebration in fellowship with the brethren, instead of a burial or memory of a funeral with mourning and sorrow. We are certainly called to rejoice in these things.

Policemen and firefighters

Without offense to anyone, we as a society make a big miration over the death of a policemen, or a firefighter because of the way they may have died, especially if they died in the line of duty, but what we don't realize is that these are only men which happen to be policemen or firemen by their choice of profession, and when they died it wasn't the policemen or the firemen which died, but a person, a parent or a sibling that we respected, loved and needed in our society, this is my point: these people deserve no more reverence and respect in death than a homeless person, we don't carry- on over a doctor like this, and their services in society are just as valuable as our public servants. If we can take into our hearts the death of a homeless person as being his time to die, then we must also take into consideration that same attitude for all people as they are simply part of the human family and say, it was his time to die, and not be partial because of his title in society. If we could just love each other then we would be able to allow them to pass off the scene with little fanfare as we do to some others. Someday we must realize that we are all here for only one great purpose and service in this life, then we must return back to the one that sent us.

Things to consider

Can you see your loved one as being put away instead of being dead?

Yes

No

How do you feel about every person being on equal footing in death? Can you make every person equal by scripture according to that which you have read?

_____

_____

If not, why not? _____

_____

_____

Let us pray

Dear heavenly Father, thank you for the comfort in death situation which the scriptures brings to our hearts in times of great stress, thank you for a reasonable period for mourning, In Jesus name. Amen!

CHAPTER VI

Slain as the prophets-Martin

How many Pastors or people of the clergy in these times in America have been slain for the word of God, as the prophets were slain in their day for righteousness sake?

It had been said that America would not elect an Irish Catholic President, not knowing that John F. Kennedy was a forerunner for Martin Luther King; as St. John the Baptist was the forerunner for Jesus. John and Robert Kennedy were Two Irish - Catholic brothers who were slain for the righteousness of the poor, and died as the prophets died for righteousness sake.

In 1963 John Kennedy was assassinated and when the news of his death broke; the world went into shock and mourned greatly for we saw our modern day hope vanish: our deliverer died; yet in a little while we were back into our daily routine.

Soon another brother: Robert Kennedy came forth to take up the fallen banner, and the same thing happened to him, and again the world went into shock and mourned for our fallen hope, yet again we were soon back into our regular routine.

There came another on the scene that was not of that immediate family who took up the charge, and died for it also, his name was Dr. Martin Luther King Jr. Martin, John and Robert Kennedy were fellow comrades in the struggle against evil; just as Jesus and His Apostles were in their day, there was Moses and David with his mighty men and Samson.

After all the time that they spent in this warfare for the world when they died we mourned little, just as it should be and we moved on with life.

History has made Jesus, Martin, The Kennedy brothers and the prophets trouble makers, and every one of them died for our struggle against evil injustices and the rights of all men, and no one seems to understand that they were soldiers in the army of the Lord; striving against evil unto blood which we have not done.

If there were ever a time or reason to mourn greatly, surely this would have been the perfect time and reason, for these people so willingly gave their lives for others right to live, and to live more abundantly in this present world.

Martin L. King's mountain top experience

Let us again look at one of our own people which we should have recognized in our lifetime, and refer to him as we compare this death and dying process to the process as we have seen it in the scriptures.

First let us find out just who was this Martin Luther King Jr, just as we had to find out who Jesus was. Martin L. King Jr. was a man that we should have realized his worth.

Like Jesus we didn't know who he was; had we known who they were would we have slain them?

It was said of Jesus, "we didn't know who He was". So we crucified Him. Just as the leadership of that day taught the people against Jesus being God come in the flesh, and taught that He was a troublemaker, and a blasphemer, history repeated itself for us, and we were taught that Martin was a troublemaker, and that he was worthy of death also.

Not once have any one of our leaders risen up, and opened our eyes to the fact that Martin **was a type** of Christ walking in the earth in our lifetime; teaching the same principles for life as Christ had taught. So we all repeated the words which were spoken in the scriptures concerning Christ, and the words were to crucify Him.

Matthew said *"and the Governor said, why, what evil hath He done? But they cried out the more, saying, let Him be crucified." Matthew 27: 23 (KJV)*

And so we did. Read Matthew 27:15-23 because like the men of old we were ignorant as to who Martin L. King Jr. was. We ignored all of his good works, and the fact that he had followers or disciples like John the Baptist and Jesus, and that he also was a man of the cloth just as our Christ was, and he fought against injustice also. Instead of calling Martin **a type of Christ and a type of apostle not the original apostle** who saw Jesus with their own eyes. (Definition for the word Apostle; the one that is first in service, one who laid the foundation of Jesus Christ, one who treaded out the uncharted territory as the Apostles laid the foundation for the truth of Jesus and the church. One who saw Jesus after His resurrection, One who saw Jesus in the flesh, and one sent forth to build upon the foundation already laid,)

Martin **was that secular apostle** persa who laid the foundation for the civil rights movement, not the original apostle as one of the twelve.

The world called Martin a civil rights leader and a troublemaker, instead of a (type) of Christ, a prophet and a modern day (type) apostle that we should follow him in his struggle for the world. Yes, we were too eager and willing to believe the negative report which we heard, because if someone had made known to us his worth we may have had no choice but to join with Martin in the battle. Maybe: just maybe some of our leaders in that day were too afraid to stand up to the challenge of facing angry ruling authority, angry prejudice people, in revealing to the world our (type) of Christ in Martin; or were they also blind leaders? But now in due time light is come that we must know and declare just who Martin was.

Yes, in retrospect we discovered that God gave to us a (type) of Christ in our lifetime; which no one recognized as our (type) of Christ in our generation. This was some serious warfare.

Yet, we repeated the cycle of death to our deliverer just as those of our past, and like Jesus, *Martin was warned by the Holy Spirit of his impending death, and Martin warned us, just as Jesus warned His disciples of His impending death.*

In the 16th chapter of the Gospel of St. John Jesus said to them: *"But now I go my way to Him that sent me; and none of you asketh me, whither goest thou? "But because I have said these things unto you, sorrow hath filled your heart. St. John 16:5, 6 (KJV)*

Also we read in another place in St. John's gospel. **Let not your heart be troubled**; *ye believe in God, believe also in me" In my Father's house are many mansions; if it were not so, I would have told you. I go to prepare a place for you." St. John 14:1, 2 (KJV)*

Envision this

This is the picture that I will paint for you: "Martin is in Memphis and he recalls being stabbed in New York City ten years before, telling them how the blade had been so close to his Aorta that if he had sneezed, the Doctor said, "he would have died".

Contrast

Here Martin is reflecting on his life and all that he would have missed had he died, just as Jesus reflected on His life, and prayed for His followers in the garden just before His death.

In St. Matthew's gospel Chapter 26 and John's Gospel Chapter 17. Martin, just as Jesus, even in the midst of all the danger that he walked in every day, yet he was glad for this time in his life. "Now" he said "It doesn't matter. It really doesn't matter what happens now." **Jesus came to that same conclusion in Matthew 26:39 when He said, "nevertheless not as I will, but as thou wilt."** Martin described the bomb threat on his plane that morning, and told how some began to talk about the threats that were out, about what would happen to him "from some of our sick brothers".

In the garden Jesus found the same strength as we hear in Martin; because the world was after His life also, only Jesus death was a must die for mankind's salvation.

In the book of Matthew 26 the ones that will kill Jesus is on their way to claim Him; but in the meanwhile in verses 38-46 He is praying that this cup would pass from Him, and like

Martin He repeats Himself, then it doesn't matter anymore, because He, like Martin just wants to do the will of God.

Well, said Martin, "I don't know what will happen now. We've got some difficult days ahead. But it really doesn't matter with me now. **Here we discern that he had gotten a word from the Lord concerning his death which brought him peace,** then he goes on to say

Because I've been to the mountain top, like anybody; I would like to live a long life: Longevity has its place, but I'm not concerned about that now. I just want to do God's will. And He's allowed me to go up to the mountain. And I've looked over. And I've seen the Promised Land. **Here we see a repeat of Moses going up on the mountain, and being able to see the Promised Land with the natural eye, but not able to enter in at that time, also this is his time and place for worship.** Deuteronomy said: *"And the Lord Spake unto Moses that selfsame day, saying," get thee up into this mountain Abarim, unto mount Nebo, which is in the land of Moab, which is over against Jericho; and behold the land of Canaan, which I give unto the children of Israel for a possession and die in the mount whither thy goest up, and be gathered unto thy people as Aaron thy brother died in mount Hor, and was gathered to his people". Deuteronomy 32:48-50 (KJV) and Deuteronomy 34. (KJV) Said: "And Moses went up from the plains of Moab unto the mountain of Nebo, to the top of Pisgah that is over against Jericho. And the Lord shewed him all the land of Gilead, unto Dan" "and all Naphtali, and the land of Ephraim, and Manasseh, and all the land of Judah, unto the utmost sea", "and the south and the plain of the valley of Jericho, the city of palm trees, unto Zoar". "And the Lord said to him, this is the land which I sware unto Abraham, unto Isaac, and unto Jacob, saying, I will give it unto thy seed; I have caused thee to see it with thine eyes, but thou shall not go over thither". "So Moses the servant of the Lord died there in the land of Moab, <u>according to the word of the Lord."</u>* ***"And He buried him in a valley in the land of Moab, over against Beth-peor; but no man knoweth of his sepulcher unto this day". "And Moses was an hundred and twenty years old when he died; his eye was not dim, nor his natural force abated".***

"And the children of Israel *wept for Moses in the plains of Moab* <u>***thirty days; so the days of weeping and mourning for Moses were ended.***</u>*" Deuteronomy 34:1-8 (KJV)*

Then Martin said; "and I may not get there with you". ***Moses didn't get there with his crew either but he made it and so will Martin.***

But I want you to know tonight that we as a people will get to the Promised Land. So I'm happy tonight. I'm not worried about anything. **Here he is comforted, and if the world had understood the urgency of his tone we would have been comforted also.** Then he goes on to say, "I'm not fearing any man, **again we see worship go up. *Hallelujah!***

"Mine eyes have seen the glory of the coming of the Lord.' *Then he turns to his faith in the Lord that He will perfect that which He promised, and He will complete the work that He has begun in him. According to Philippians 1:6 (KJV)*

Many who heard the "Mountaintop" speech were convinced that King had had a premonition of death or as we might say: an epiphany. Young thought it "almost morbid" and others worried about its tone of resignation and impending doom.

Like Jesus the threats of death was heavy on his life. But, Martin had the same heart as Jesus had in the garden.

In Matthew 26 the scriptures said that Jesus prayed the same prayer three times, that was, that this cup would pass from Him; **finally after wrestling with the notion of death,** He reconciled Himself to the Fathers will. "I want to live," Martin kept saying. Yet he took consolation in the fact that history would go on if he died, (and this is the most important thing that we must understand and embrace); it doesn't matter which of us die" whether it be mother, father, sister, brother, infant or toddler life goes on and we must carry on as never before because now we understand loss, and can now appreciate life more than ever before.

This is truly the time and place for us to worship God. Because he had finally reconciled himself to the will of the Lord the anxiety that had bothered Martin that day was now gone.

This is what the church should already know, and teach to the saints: that they have no time to suffer the lost as hard, and as long as we do today.

After we have wrestled with the notion of death, then are we able to reconcile ourselves to the will of God in death without fear.

For Martin, it was six o'clock time to go to dinner, but instead shots rang out and Martin was down," Oh my God" cried Abernathy" Martin's been shot! (Now is the time for that old familiar spirit to take his place, Panic, fear, shock and disbelief. This is that enemy that we are trying to eradicate when death strikes.) Kyles found himself in Room 306, **screaming into the telephone in a futile attempt to get the operator, banging his head again and again against the wall. Here we see torment.** Bernard Lee was beside him now, **dumb from shock.** The time of death was recorded at 7:05 p.m. April 4, 1968.

Although Martin's body wasn't cold yet; Eskridge said, "You have to become our leader. You are now our leader. Yes, they chose a leader right on the spot a reminder just as Aaron's sons took his place before the act of death occurred, and as Joshua took Moses place before Moses death occurred, even though he may be a substitute for someone else, hooray they **are getting immediately back into life; and continuing to carry out the work** of Martin's ministry without hesitation.

Without a word, Abernathy reached out with his arms, and the three men came together; they hugged each other and wept with their faces together, *then Abernathy said a prayer for the King, this is where they found their place of worship.*

Then Eskridge and Young each took him by the arm and helped him out the door to face the din of reporters.

Excerpts taken from the book: Let the trumpet sound
The life: of Martin Luther King, JR.
Written by Stephen B. Oates
And all scriptures are taken from the Kings James version of the Bible.

Question:

How did you receive the contrast between Martin and Jesus?

_____

_____

Did you see martin's work as unto the Lord?

Yes, explain you answer. _____

_____

No, explain your answer_____

_____

In your opinion was Martin a type of Christ in his duties? Explain your answer.

_____

_____

_____

_____

_____

Let us look at another of our own in our lifetime.

Excellent example of death's grasp on us

Let me give you this true story as an example as to how we let death withhold us from moving on in whatever area of life, that we should be presently functioning in.

While I was in the midst of preparing this study on death and dying our lady congress-woman of Indianapolis, Indiana died. We had the warning that the Holy Spirit gives to us in these circumstances. The Congresswoman had been off and on in her career, and her public knew well that she was ill, even her appearance told a story in itself. Yet, the people of the city carried on as if all was well, and she would return to her position in life, then one day the news came that the lady had terminal cancer: Of course the traffic began; after that they presented to the public what the people called a candlelight vigil: I don't think that anyone realized it, but this was actually a living memorial to her, not a prayer vigil.

At that time the radio station WTLC gave her public a platform that the people could call in and express what was in their hearts as to what difference she had made in their lives. Many prayers went up on her behalf so that she could hear all the wonderful comments and gratitude which were expressed concerning her service to many souls, her public was saying in her ear well done. <u>But the one and only great purpose for the great lady's life had been fulfilled,</u> and the call of death from God was heard by her and she responded to its call, then came the news that the lady was dead. On this particular day there was snow on the ground and we were expecting a blizzard, yet, we all came out to this weekly Concerned Clergy's meeting because it was said in the week prior to be important, so here we were when the news came that the lady had died.

What do you supposed happened next?

Let me tell you what happened; some of the people began to weep, please, don't misunderstand it was ok to weep and understandably so, but the weepers were the leaders. Pastors and Preachers and **not the lay people,** the one's that should have set the standard, and should have known to, and how to restrain themselves and continue on in the business at hand, as some of the people which we have seen in the scriptures had to do, such as Aaron had to do concerning his sons death.

But instead, I saw the Pastors and Preachers weeping; these which should have been our strength they became the weak link before the eyes of the lay members: and caused the meeting to cease when others which were lay people, knew that we should continue on in this business at hand. And some spoke about us as being weak leadership, for the people do watch us and normally they follow our lead in this case they didn't.

Question

Why do we suppose they responded in such a manner? Some thought it was in respect for her demise, others thought that the state had lost a great warrior, and others thought that it was right to rush to comfort the family; and others thoughts weren't so pure, for the climbers this was a great opportunity for them to be recognized as one of the first to be on the scene, even in the news cameras that their names might be mentioned.

They readily forgot that she would have been the first to say **"move on and let's get it done"** the ministers didn't know the ways of death and dying according to the scriptures, because they themselves had not been taught, nor do they realize that this teaching must come forth to the people beginning with them.

A few days later we attended her wake and funeral it was quite beautiful and something to be remembered just as it should have been, and many wonderful words were spoken concerning her, but we heard and saw little weeping, because the people had pretty much accepted her death, this is the way it should be in death we must weep briefly, but we must celebrate the life lived whole heartily.

Do you agree that the Pastors should have been our examples of how to respond to the news of her death?

Yes

No

Unsure?

Do you agree with a living memorial?

_____

_____

_____

Have you made preparation and arrangements for you eventful day?

Yes

No

If not, why not?

Do you plan to make your wishes known, or will you leave it to others?

2008 summer Olympiad

World event

Our people who are in leadership positions don't always lead in a positive way in times of their testing. Why? Because they have not been schooled in the correct mind set of death and dying, and how they should respond to such, especially if no example has been spoken or demonstrated before them.

Example

What if the coach who lost his father in-law during the time of the Olympic Games had been in a position which would have required him to remain on his post or lose his job? Just like Aaron and his sons, when his sons and their brothers were killed by the Lord for the offering of strange fire. What do you suppose would have been his response?

I remember one coach who knew exactly what his duties and responsibilities were to his team and to society when his son committed suicide. This man became an excellent example that we all should follow. He faithfully remained on his post, and carried out his duties as a coach without hesitation while he was in the midst of his suffering, and all that came with it. Well done!

CHAPTER VII

Martyr

Now that we have read in the scriptures how Abraham, Jacob, Job, Aaron, Jesus, Martin and others dealt with death and dying: let us move on to appreciate the death of the apostles who brought to us the one and only doctrine that we all as Christians should follow.

In Matthew's gospel Jesus is talking with His disciples, and He said to them; *"He that receiveth you (the apostles) receives me, and he that receiveth me receiveth Him that sent me. (The Father) he that receiveth a prophet in the name of a prophet shall receive a prophet's reward; and he that receiveth a righteous man in the name of a righteous man shall receive a righteous man reward."* Matthew 10:40, 41 (KJV)

St. John's gospel said, *"Neither pray I for these alone, but for them also which **shall believe on me through their word"**. (The apostles)* St. John 17:20 (KJV)

Then came the martyrdom of the one's which caused us to believe, yet some of them like Martin, John, and Jesus, gladly gave their lives for our cause, and we saw them go off the scene in death. We not realizing that they were our delivers in our generation.

Here are some others which have laid down their lives in the war against evil for our sakes, and if the mourning process should be lengthy then these are the ones that deserve our lengthy mourning. Not only should we grieve for our loss of them, but also for how tragically they died for this cause.

The martyred ones

First, we have Stephen and Nicanor great deacons suffered martyrdom Stephen the deacon, being stoned to death, for the sake of the gospel; and died asking God to forgive them. (His murderers)

Apostle James the Great, the son of Zebedee the elder brother of John, was beheaded cheerfully. A.D 44

Phillip the Evangelist, after much ministry was, scourged, thrown into prison, and afterward crucified. A.D 54

Matthew the Apostle, suffered martyrdom, being slain with a halberd in the city of Nadabah, A.D 60

James the Less, at the age of ninety four he was beat and stoned by the Jews; and finally had his brains bashed out with a fuller's club.

Matthias the Apostle that took the place of Judas. Was stoned at Jerusalem and then beheaded.

Andrew the Apostle the brother of Peter, was crucified on a cross, the two ends of which were fixed transversely in the ground. This gave us the term, St. Andrews's cross.

St. Mark a companion was dragged to pieces by the people of Alexandria, at the great solemnity of Serapis their idol, ending his life under their merciless hands.

Peter the Apostle, but, coming to the gate, he saw the Lord Christ come to meet him, to whom he, worshipping, said, Lord, whither dost thou go?

To whom He answered and said, "I am come again to be crucified" by this, Peter, perceiving His suffering to be understood, returned into the city, Jerome saith that he was crucified, his head being down and his feet upward, himself so requiring, because he was (he said) unworthy to be crucified after the same form and manner as the Lord Jesus.

Paul the Apostle, they, coming to Paul instructing the people, desired him to pray for them, that they might believe; who told them shortly after they should believe and be baptized at his sepulcher. This done, the soldiers came and led him out of the city to the place of execution, where he, after his prayers made, gave his neck to the sword.

Apostle Judas the brother of James, was commonly called Thaddeus; he was crucified at Edessa, A.D 72.

Apostle Bartholomew, preached in several countries, and having translated the gospel of Matthew into the language of India, he was at length cruelly beaten and then crucified by the impatient idolaters.

Apostle Thomas called Didymus, preached the gospel in Parthia and India, where exciting the rage of the pagan priests, he was martyred by being thrust through with a spear.

Luke the evangelist, was the author of the gospel which goes under his name and Acts; he traveled with Paul through various countries, and is suppose to have been hanged on an olive tree, by the idolatrous priests of Greece.

Apostle Simon surnamed Zelotes preached in Mauritania, Africa, and even in Britain, in which latter country he was crucified, A.D. 74

John the "Beloved disciple," was brother to James the great, the churches of Smyrna, Pergamos, Sardis, Philadelphia, Laodicea, and Thyatira, were founded by him. From Ephesus he was ordered to be sent to Rome, where it is affirmed that he was cast into a cauldron of boiling oil. He escaped by Miracle, without injury. Domitian afterwards banished him to the Isle of Patmos, where he wrote the book of Revelation. Nerva, the successor of Domitian, recalled him. He was the only Apostle who escaped a violent death.

All these died and there is no mention of anyone now or then that is in bereavement for these apostles, yet we are bereaved for our family members whether they are good and productive to society or not. Let all men be in the same category when it comes to death, for we live then we die.

These excerpts were taken from the Foxes book of martyrs

CHAPTER VIII

End of the subject?

Ecclesiastes brings to mind the thought that there is a time and purpose to every thing.

To everything there is a season, and a time to every purpose under the heaven. Ecclesiastes 3:1(KJV)

We will use some of these words to bring to life the process that we must understand and practice.

The Wisdom of Solomon said that there is a time to be born, <u>and a time to die.</u> If this be the case why do we grieve so hard when one dies, and why does the period of grief last so long.

My Answer?

Mainly because of a lack of education and instruction from the word of God concerning this subject, he also said that there is <u>a time to weep,</u> weeping is something that we all do at some point in life, but mourning goes far above weeping to the point that the spirit of mourning, and the spirit of grief will take over, and hold us captive for years; so there is a period to mourn and then mourning must cease before the spirit of grief takes his seat in our lives, as saints we should have already heard these words, and these words should already have applied themselves to our hearts.

Um tell me more, tell me more

This could be the end of this subject but why stop here, when there is so much more to speak about on the subject of death and dying good and bad. This is where we are suppose to take these words to heart; the words which are given to us in the book of 1ˢᵗ Thessalonians 4:13-18 (KJV) which said, "*Verse 13 but I would not have you to be ignorant, brethren, concerning them **which are asleep**"*, did you hear that? The word said they are asleep.

Speaking of the saints that died in Christ, and have a hope in Jesus that they will rise one day to hear the **words** *"well done thy good and faithful servant, you have been faithful over few things come up hither I will make you ruler over many."* then it speaks on the negative side; that ye sorrow not as those that have no hope.

The saints are not to be in sorrow and grief as the heathen which have no hope of the first resurrection. (Having no hope is to be without Christ) *Verse 14 said, for if we believe that Jesus died and rose again, even so them also which sleeps in Jesus will God bring with Him.*

This is our hope that we will see this person again, if that person and yourself are in Christ,

This person is not really dead but only asleep, living, at rest and happy.

Verse 15. For this we say unto you **by the word of the Lord,** (not by how we think things ought to be done; nor by our emotions), but according to the word of the Lord is what we must trust and do. Then it goes on to say that:

We which are alive and remain unto the coming of the Lord shall not prevent them which **are asleep.**

'Here we find that we lose no one, we are all here together in His good care, hallelujah!

Verse 16 said. For the Lord Himself shall descend from Heaven with a shout, with the voice of the arch-angel, and with the trump of God; and the dead in Christ shall rise first; then we which are alive and remain shall be caught up together with them in the clouds, to meet the Lord in the air; and so shall we ever be with the Lord.

Verse 18 said wherefore comfort one another with these words.

These are the instructions which we are commanded to use in times of death, yet we use everything else, and not what is given to us according to the word of the Lord that we may have peace in the midst of sorrow.

The church must first teach the members how to be comforted which encourages the heart; this will cause men to worship and not to mourn and grieve.

Personal experience

If I may use some of my own personal experiences which I rarely do, but this experience happened to me while I was a child.

I had a sister who died when I was very young, she was the most beautiful child that any of us had ever laid our eyes on, and we heard that statement from every one that saw her and she rarely cried. Her name was Delfelia and every one thought that an angel had been sent down from heaven because of her beauty.

After about three months of life; we were awaken in the early morning hours with the sound of a frantic cry from our mother, which said "My baby ain't breathing! O Lord! My baby is dead!"

Then came the sobs, normally the baby slept in between them, only this time the baby slept on the outside of mother. Next I heard my stepfather say "you must have laid on her" and mother said "no I didn't" Of course they wouldn't allow us (the children) in the room. We didn't know about SIDS at that time, so when the Doctor arrived and examined the body he didn't say suffocation, he did say "I don't know the cause of death".

So it wasn't suffocation, but Sid's which we learned of later in life.

Here are several things we should notice.

- We experienced our first death in our immediate family
- We heard weeping
- We heard accusation
- Then we heard guilt and blame
- Finally the funeral and the committal

In retrospect as a child this is what I remember, I was reminded that the children weren't crying about this death, and this child was child number four, so we as the older ones weren't babes, but when our mother wept we wept. So the weeping was projected onto the children by the older ones who was weeping; the children weren't weeping on their own they accepted the natural process. The same thing happened when my grandmother died in 1971 the weeping of the adults was projected onto the children causing them to weep also.

When my husband's niece was suddenly shot and killed, all of her siblings were outraged; every time the pangs of death overwhelmed them, and their thoughts of her being dead the bawling began afresh, because they couldn't understand why this agony was so overwhelming, and just wouldn't leave them alone, or why it kept assaulting them in spurts, or in waves.

Note:

This young woman had a three year old daughter who didn't shed a tear, but when one of the other children began to weep they would always reach out and embrace her, and say to her "your mama is dead, that girl killed your mama". This is the type of projection that I am speaking about, other people's grief being passed one to another even when they have no desire to weep, this weeping is expected of us by others.

Question:

How do you suppose we should respond to death and dying?

My answer

We should respond to this event as a little child, not because we don't love our people, or that we are cold hearted, but because God has given to us the way to respond to life and living as well as death and dying.

Living memorial

I personally would love to have a living memorial before my death like our congress-woman. I surely appreciate the concept which my sister Marnett brought to my heart, and actually seeing it happen with our congress-woman made it a service to be desired. Though my sister said she wanted to have a living memorial, she in her good moments didn't really believe that death was so near, because she could draw her next breath she kept putting it off that we weren't able to have that living memorial for her, because she simply ran out of time.

She was a person who had ovarian cancer and sometimes was very ill, at other times she was in pretty good spirit; every time she was in one of her bad periods of pain and agony she would remember that death was rapidly approaching, and that she wanted to have a living Memorial, but as soon as the pain would cease or diminish she would forget the thought of a living memorial (Dying).

These periods of pain were her warning, and her reminders of death which she continued to ignore. This just prove that even when a person is dying he or she thinks as long as they can draw that next breath that he or she has a future; and whatever needs to be done today can be put off until tomorrow, and too soon today is gone and there is no tomorrow there is only yesterday. Soon she was dead and now we must have some type of service in her memory, because she didn't want a traditional funeral, but a cremation service which meant having no corpse present; then came the time for her memorial service, and many of the family members especially the young men (nephews) wept bitterly as they spoke of their time spent with her in this life, as some of the others looked on and saw the agony of the ones which spoke, that caused them to greatly weep and it became a chained reaction in the weeping process.

There were no tears for me, even while I was watching the others weep and agonize in their grief. I had never seen it like this before: this truly was a learning experience for me. Their mourning and grief did not project onto me to weep at that time or afterward. I didn't know personally until later that it was possible not to weep at all; **because of this preparation**.

Thank God, because I already had this word in my inward parts, and because I had asked the Lord if he would cause me to never be bereaved, I never in all of the days of my life wanted to be bereaved, and so I was not bereaved then, nor am I bereaved now, even until this day though I was in a bereaved family. Thank you Lord

Question:

Should adults follow the example of children in this death process?
Yes, explain your answer_____

_____

_____

Maybe not? Explain your answer

_____

_____

_____

What other approach would you recommend in this process?

_____

_____

_____

Can you offer any suggestions on how to let go of bereavement?

_____

_____

_____

Express your heart here

CHAPTER IX

The negative side of death

We have looked at the positive side of death and dying, now let us hear what is said and done in the negative side of death and dying, especially in the negative side of dying.

We must continue to refer to the scriptures instead of the old ways of our forefathers. (Tradition) denominational tradition said that we should not take nonbelievers into the church for his or her funeral after he or she is dead, because he or she had made a conscious decision in life not to attend the church while he or she were yet alive.

However, I caution the church leaders to understand that the words of comfort is not directed toward the dead, and the funeral is not about the dead or whether or not he or she was a believer, but the message, and the process of the ceremony is to the living who also may not have gone to church in the past for whatever reason, this word of God being preached in this type of environment could direct these nonbelievers who attended the church for this purpose to salvation; because of this body being in the church environment after their death. Remember, the church is the saints in the body of Christ, and not the building where we go to worship.

Again, the scripture is still our only source that we must refer to for comfort no matter what the circumstances may be.

Ecclesiastes 7:17-B (KJV) asks us the question. *Why should you die before your time?*

*Verse 17 said for us to be not over much wicked, neither be thou foolish, why **shouldest thou die before thy time?***

We think our bounds are set to die. Yet, the scripture asked the question why should you die **before your time?**

The question itself leads us to believe that somehow we must be able to shorten our days, this let us know that somewhere in our lives there must be something that we must do in order to shorten our days. The act of disobedience to parents is a major cause. Ephesians 6:1-3 (KJV) *"The fear of the Lord prolongeth days; but the years of the wicked shall be shortened."* Proverbs 10:27(KJV) **Bloody and deceitful men shall not live out half of their days.**

But thou, O God, shalt bring them down into the pit of destruction; <u>bloody and deceitful men shall not live out half their days;</u> but I will trust in thee. Psalm 55:23 (KJV) let us begin to look at foolishness on the negative side of death.

I would like to tell you of an incident that happened in my lifetime, one that I can actually give witness to as the Apostles gave witness to the gospel of Jesus Christ; it is not something that I heard about but it was a tragedy that I know of personally.

There was a young woman who belonged to this church: because of the things that were going on in this church where the Saints weren't saved, and the fact that she wasn't learning anything there, because the teaching was shallow, and we never got the Holy Ghost in that place, she dropped out, left home and the church. Things soon got hard for her living on her own, because she was trying to support a man that he might love her: so she had to return back to her mother's home. Since she had returned to her mothers' home, her mother insisted that she return to the church which happened to be this same church. Yes, this is the same church where the saint's weren't saved. The same place where I had to return to over and over.

Naturally she wasn't happy. So she would come to church every Sunday, but she would not enter into the sanctuary, she consistently sat in the hallway doing the entire service.

One day after the break-up of the relationship with this man, who had dropped her for another woman who worked in the same work place as she did, and the fact that he was still getting money from her to spend on this woman, this young woman had a pretty face, but she was somewhat over weight, and he had said as much to her that she was fat.

The fact that her family knew that she was being played, and the fact that she just couldn't let go was too much for her to cope with; her self-esteem was already low, and his words caused her self-esteem to be completely destroyed.

The spirit of no return

One day she began to communicate before them her thoughts of killing herself.

As serious as she was about her intentions, she would say it with a smile as if she was kidding yet with determination.

<u>"Even on the negative side of death we hear the warning of death"</u>

She told her family members several times that she was going to kill herself, at one point she took a hand full of pills; apparently they weren't strong enough to do the job, or maybe it just wasn't her time of departure, and no one intervened. Yet, she continued in her efforts to destroy herself only this time she bought a gun. This girl's pain was so intense and so deep within her that she simply couldn't cope. While her pain was much too great for her to bear, her loneliness was even more extreme in the deep part of her soul, even her embarrassment was too overwhelming for her to contain it within herself.

Finally the day came that she was to carry out her plan of her death, that's when she began sending text messages to her family members across the city, and in other States saying her goodbyes. At this point family members began to plead with her not to do such a thing, but no one called the police to have her detained for intervention, even if it happened to be a false alarm. (We are bound by the law to call the police in these cases.)

This time they knew that it was too late to stop her from committing this act they felt the fear, and the helplessness within themselves and they knew that this time it was the real thing.

After she had said all of her goodbyes she went home, and sent her fourteen year old son (which actually belonged to someone else who wouldn't do their job as a parent) to her mothers' house so she could be alone, even then she told him, I quote, "go over to mama's house because I don't want to hurt you". After he had left the house the report came that she had shot herself. But there is still a question in my mind; was she really trying to kill herself, or was she still crying out for help? You see, she shot herself in a place that wouldn't typically kill a person; she shot herself in her midriff the area where most people typically recover.

This is speculation on my part. But do you suppose that maybe she thought this act would cause this man to return to her, and maybe even cause him to love her? Well, the bullet traveled through her body and struck an artery, after a while she died because they couldn't stop her flow of blood. Now in comes that spirit of fear, grief, shock, Sorrow, panic, weeping, shame, guilt and self blame.

This is where the family really needed the word of God to have already been instilled, or applied to their hearts concerning death and dying, even though this type of death still would have crushed them to their very core. The Spirit of God through His word would have had a greater opportunity to work in them to heal, more than the spirit of no hope would have had to ravish them.

This is truly the negative side of death.

It seems that after a few days had gone by the Pastor of that church still had not gone to comfort nor to counsel the family; of course I didn't know that until I went to offer my condolences, that's when they informed me that he had not approached them at all neither had any other minister of that particular church. I learned all these facts while communicating with the immediate family, the mother.

My family and I were no longer members of that church and I had no reason to return there, and I had not seen them for awhile, so I didn't visit them right away. I assumed the Pastor and the church members would be rallying around them as they should have, and I would really be in the way and out of place, but it was just the opposite. I kept hearing in my spirit to go, and offer your condolences and comfort, still I didn't go right away because I felt like I would be an uninvited guest in such a painful hour. I also felt that I would have been running ahead of their Pastor concerning his sheep.

Constantly I kept hearing the Spirit saying to me you have known these people for over twenty years can you put aside all of the past, and not feel like an intruder and go and minister to them for me? So I went. But I wouldn't go alone: I took my little boy and my husband with me, and when we arrived at this woman's home this woman was so glad to hear from us, and to see anyone that would come to offer them any words of comfort and support.

It is truly a glorious thing to me: that God have a will for our lives, and that he can cause any one of us to submit to His will without harm or anguish. Actually the Lord shamed me without pain.

The same words, and the instruction of God is for the living, and not the dead, to unite families and to call sinners to salvation

The Spirit of comfort

First I embraced her with a strong hug, and in return she responded in the same manner; she held me so long and so tight, that I knew I couldn't just come and say how sorry I was that this tragic incident had happen to them and walk away, it became necessary for me to go beyond the bounds that I thought were there.

So she invited us into her home, and she talked with us and told us all about this thing; even as we sat there the waves of panic, guilt and anxiety kept crashing in on her like the ocean's waves dashing against the rocks. Every time the thought of what had happened came to her, guilt would show up and this woman was bowed down in her pain. As I watched her I began to speak to her concerning her pain. I said to her "don't fight the pain, let the pain in to have its way" again, I said to her "every time the waves come let them flow over you, don't stop the waves" and she said "how do you know that the waves keep coming?" And I said to her "I can see them hitting you, and that she was not to fight them nor was she to resist them, because these pains were pains of healing, these pains were like labor pains, and every time she stopped the pain she had to deal with that pain again, because it had not accomplished its purpose" So I said to her "let the pain come that it may pass through and not return".

As we sat there she kept telling us her story, and her guilt and shame was far worse than any part of the act that was committed.

Giving counsel to the bereaved

Somehow I was able to tell her that when people have purposed a thing in there hearts for whatever reason, that they have a tendency to somehow give us the slip, and how hopeless we feel when things happen that's so tragic and that it was not her fault.

After a while I called all the family members that were in the house together; and asked each one of them to expound upon their feelings concerning this tragedy which had occurred in their family. I was surprised that I didn't have to coax them to come; they came and spoke freely and willingly. This gave each of them an opportunity to respond to their bewilderment and grief, and it gave the other members of the family an opportunity to hear how, and what each of the other individuals thought and felt.

After that we had prayer, not my prayers alone, but my husband's prayers, and then each one of them had to say their own personal prayer no matter how brief they were, even the mother prayed, and we said the prayers in rounds, then we sang songs as if we were having church, at that point the Spirit changed the atmosphere some what. (Here, and unknowingly we had come to the place of worship)

I didn't realize it at that moment, but I was bringing them to the place of worship that I didn't know at that time that we should do, and I didn't know it because of a lack of biblical teaching.

It was God in the midst of this tragedy showing us what we should do in these hopeless situations; it took me quite sometime to understand what God did in the midst of us that day,

It shouldn't have taken me so long to understand what God was doing with us: it should have been obvious, because I had no knowledge of what was supposed to take place in these situations; I simply followed the Holy Spirit which caused all of us to worship in the mist of the worse kind of pain.

These people saw this death as one of their own being lost and without hope forever. Again, I say that it took the same word; and the same God in this situation as any other saved or unsaved. God compelled me to go and minister to people that had no use for me. Yet, God chose me again with these same people who hated me, because He needed someone to respond to Him in the mist of the grief of death and dying: just as Moses did concerning his family. God needed someone to bring words of comfort to the family from the correct source which is the scriptures, even in what seems like a hopeless situation, especially to those that have no hope of seeing their family member again. It is the same word of God toward the family members that we must use at the funeral: whether the dead be saved or whether the dead be dammed.

A day or so later I went to this woman's sister's home with a different group of family members, and we repeated these steps all over again in Jesus name. But while I was at this woman's home one of the Preachers from their church finally came to counsel them, but it was a long time before he came to minister to them, but God wouldn't let him arrive until we were about finished. It was God who had sent me ahead of him because of the service which had to be performed, and because He had to teach me the things that no Preacher had taught me, and because of the revelation which He would reveal unto me; concerning the actions that should be taken in all cases of death and dying.

Had this Minister shown up ahead of me I'm sure he would have prayed, but maybe he would not have taken it to the next level which was to bring the family to worship. As David, Job, Moses, and Abraham did, because he didn't know that worship is what we are called to do in these trying times, and it would not have happened because he never knew to do it, why? Because the Pastor never taught it to the congregation, because no one had ever taught it to him.

Returning back and his great question

Afterward the Holy Spirit placed a strong unction on me to go back to the home of the bereaved mother. So I returned back to their home to speak to the deceased woman's fourteen year old son, and he spoke with me privately, openly and without hesitation: because he had questions, this was a serious and painful time for him.

But his great question to me was "will my mother go to Hell? Seriously, if I had known the answer to be without a doubt emphatically yes, I would not have told him. Why not?

First, he was much too young to have to deal with such permanent matters, at this point he himself felt too helpless and disconnected. Secondly, he was much too vulnerable for an affirmative answer he already wanted to die. Thirdly, I would have sentenced this woman to a certain place without positive proof as to where she was.

So, the Spirit of God quickened me to ask him a question, I asked him "did your mother die right away? And he said "no" then I told him that we didn't know if she repented or not, or if she was conscious enough to repent to God or not, and that she was in the hands of the Lord, and it was up to God in His mercy whether she would enter into heaven or not.

This is where sensitivity is a must: we at this point could cause irreparable harm to another soul if we say the wrong things, even if they are true according to the scriptures.

Time and teaching will cause all of us to reach the correct conclusion concerning, whether or not our loved one's made it into the kingdom of God.

This is the time when bereavement presents special Pastoral care opportunities.

The day of the funeral arrived, and the family not only had anger in their hearts toward the Pastor for his negligence, but they became more incensed when he stood over the pulpit, and informed every one of the unfortunate circumstance under which this young woman had died.

I tell you, the Pastor was trying so desperately to offer this family a comforting explanation as to how this woman would fair in the afterlife now that she had committed suicide, but this was the one thing that they had tried so desperately to conceal from the ears of the public, and the Pastor just blurted it out in his carnal attempt to comfort them.

This was not done with malice but it hurt, and embarrassed the family just as bad as if it had been intentional.

This is where discretion is advised by the word of God and not by our emotions to comfort.

Here we see anguish increased in them, because now they are embarrassed, because so many of us damn a person to hell for this act, now the word is gone out that this young woman who had been in church for years had taken her own life.

At this funeral some family members saw fit to make her a prophet calling her a woman of God; so all the people that attended that funeral heard and saw the anguish, pain and agony in that place that no words could comfort them, because they could only hear their pain, anger and sorrow speaking to them through the voice of the spirit of no hope.

What a sorrowful ending to a life which God Himself died for, this is what happens when we trust in the flesh and not in God.

This young woman died at the age of 34 years of a self inflicted gunshot wound.

Ezekiel 18:4, 20 (KJV) said that all souls are mine… this tells us that no person has a right to take one's own life, because it belongs to God alone.

But this story became the epitaph of her life and legacy. After all of this the family still had to carry on without her.

What could you have added to the process to recover in this situation without the word of God?

_____

_____

_____

How should the Pastor have responded to the family in this situation?

_____

_____

_____

Was the Pastor negligent in his duties?

_____

_____

What would have been your reaction to this negligence had this been your family and church?

_____

_____

Would you have remained a member of that church?

_____

Yes

No

If you had left that church would you have told the Pastor why you were leaving?

Yes

No

Expound on you emotions, then rethink logically and write some positive answers as to what you should do spiritually.

CHAPTER X

Current Events, Despondent

Currently we are seeing to many young people commit suicide. After one person commits suicide it seems that others soon become despondent and wants to die also, as her son wanted to get out of life because he felt like he couldn't cope, and death would be simpler and easier than living, the act of suicide in many cases causes a chain reaction especially in young people.

Again the spirit of guilt causes others to feel as if they didn't do their best for this person. If we as teachers would begin to teach the people about self-worth and the value of life early, and that Jesus died for all the people and He sees none of us as worthless, and that He will forgive all sin. Murders, thieves, liars, whores, homosexuality and the like, then maybe We would have more of a success rate in saving our people from condemning themselves to an early grave, because of a temporary situation; know this, things will soon change hold-on! Don't give up.

Suicide is forever, yet preventable:

Most people who consider suicide do not want to die- they just want their pain to go away.

If you know someone that may want to commit suicide, here are some things you may be able to do to help

Be direct. Talk openly and matter-of - factly about suicide.
Be willing to listen. Allow expression of feelings and accept the feelings.
Get involved. Be available. Show interest and support.
Offer hope that other alternatives are available, but no glib reassurance.
Take action. Remove means such as guns or pills.
Offer compassion.

Things not to do:

Do not be judgmental. Do not debate whether suicide is right or wrong.
Do not lecture on the value of life.
Do not act shocked. This will put distance between you and the person at risk.
Do not leave the person alone if you believe the risk is immediate.
Do not counsel the person yourself.
But do get help from persons or agencies specializing in crisis intervention and suicide prevention in your town.
Excerpts are taken from our local help line.

Let us look further at the negative side of death

Jesus asked the question in Mark's gospel

"For what shall it profit a man, if he shall gain the whole world, and lose his own soul?

Mark 8:36 (KJV)

Ezekiel tells us to warn the wicked so they don't end up outside of the gate. Ezekiel 3:17-21(KJV)

When I say unto the wicked, thou shall surely die; and thou givest him not warning, nor speakest to warn the wicked from his wicked way, to save his life; the same wicked man shall die in his iniquity; but his blood will I require at thine hand. Yet if thou warn the wicked and he turn not from his wickedness, nor from his wicked way, he shall die in his iniquity; but thou hast delivered thy soul. Ezekiel 3:18, 19 (KJV)

These scriptures show to us the warning of not only death, but how we will fare in death. Ezekiel 33:7-11(KJV)

Included on the negative side of death and dying we must warn the people by the word of God. According to the scriptures.

The negative side of dying

There is definitely a negative side of death and dying, and we should instruct our people in the knowledge of the negative as well as the positive, and to encourage our loved ones to **choose life in every situation: choose life.**

We realize that all things come from God and that all things must return back to God. Yet, there are people who determine in their own minds that all things come from themselves. *But we found in 1ˢᵗ Thessalonians 4.*

*For the **Lord Himself** shall descend from heaven with a shout, with the voice of the archangel, and with the trump of God; and the dead in Christ shall rise first, then we which are alive and remain shall be caught up together with them in the clouds, to meet the Lord in the air; and so we shall ever be with the Lord. 1ˢᵗ Thessalonian 4:16, 17(KJV)*

Which means that the wicked, the fearful and the unbelieving shall be left in the grave until, after God has dealt with the sinners which remain on the earth, and then they must stand together before the great white throne of judgment, this is where the wicked, the fearful and the unbelieving will be judged by God, and there, they will be cast into the lake of fire and brimstones where there will be weeping and gnashing of teeth. Revelation 20: 11-15 (KJV)

But the fearful, and unbelieving, and the abominable, and murders, and whoremongers, and sorcerers, and idolaters, and all liars, shall have their part in the lake which burneth with fire and brimstone; which is the second death. Revelation 21:8 (KJV)

This is how we know how our loved ones will fair after their death, whether they go to heaven or hell according to their living, according to the scriptures. We see an excellent demonstration of this fire of torment in the next few verses of scripture.

We will find that the rich man in Luke's gospel gave us a conversation being heard in the place of his abode after his death, but it gave no reference of anyone weeping or mourning for this particular person. But we did fine the rich man in much torment and no comfort is ever to be found for him, at this point even the scriptures can't help anyone that is in his position, there is such a time as too late. Read Luke 16: 19- 31 (KJV)

Man lost

This is our example of a person who gained the world and lost his soul. Again, in Luke's gospel we recognize the rich man without a savior; this is definitely a Negative.

I am reasonably sure that he had heard about Jesus in his lifetime, and rejected Him as so many have heard in our lifetime, and have rejected the word which they have heard.

In Luke's gospel the rich man had everything and Lazarus had nothing, but someone lay Lazarus at the rich man's gate every day full of sores, yet the rich man never showed to Lazarus charity, nor did he cause his servants to bind up Lazarus wounds.

As it reads in Luke's Gospel

"And there was a certain rich man, which was clothed in purple and in fine linen; and fared sumptuously every day; and there was a certain beggar named Lazarus, And desiring to be fed with the crumbs from the rich mans table; moreover the dogs licked his sores. And it came to pass that the beggar died and was carried by the Angles into Abraham's bosom; (paradise) the rich man died also and was buried; and in HELL he lift up his eyes and being in torments, seeth Abraham afar off, and Lazarus in his bosom.

(This is surely the ultimate negative side of death)

*And he cried and said, Father Abraham, have mercy on me, and send Lazarus that he may dip the tip of his finger in water, and cool my tongue; for **I am tormented in this flame.** Luke 16:19- 24 (KJV)*

Now the rich man sees Lazarus afar off in the place of peace and comfort, but the rich man finds himself in a place of torment. This is where we should have a season of great sorrowful mourning, not because of death; but because a soul has been lost to Hell forever, and yet, even in this type of mourning, mourning must soon cease.

All the reference given was of the rich man's living, and when his life was over no one seemed to remember him. This is why the Clergy and parents must teach salvation to the people of the world, beginning with our own family members, because there will come a time when we all will have to deal with death in some fashion in our lifetime; whether it be the death of a family member or friend, or our very own death, even in death this ministry must continue.

The world loving their own

The three cases which readily come to mind are, Ms. Diana, Michael, and Elvis Presley. I pray that no one will take offense at my words: but, this is to understand the message of death and dying, some compared to others. Mrs. Diana, died and the world was in such shock because of her sudden death, because they loved her and her lifestyle, but somehow the world only remembered the glory of her life, and forgot the final activities of her life, and the sorrow of where she may wake up in the afterlife; but people wept so hard because of her death that they came from around the globe just to be in the same space as she was in: even though she was dead. There were flowers galore and wall to wall people, there were also a need for crowd control, because the people didn't want her to be put away; this hurt them so much they couldn't believe that this was so, and yes; every year there is a crowd gathered together in her memory. This woman was in the news daily until she was put in the grave; after that, and even now there is much to do about Miss Diana.

This is my question, why is there so much A-do over the worldly people compared to the Godly soul saving people?

Does anyone remember mother Teresa? She was that woman who lived such a lowly life. She was the one that went everywhere, and gave her time and her life to the work of the ministry for the lost and suffering souls. She was the one who held dying children in her arms, praying for their relief in such places where they would receive no medicine or services.

This is the woman which died in the same time frame as Miss Diana; who was out of the ground for quite some time, but mother Teresa was put away very quickly because of her circumstances; but not many people had the same interest in her life and work as so many did with Miss Diana, especially the media. Mother didn't have a huge number of flowers and a flock of people as Miss Diana. And the world soon put mother away in their hearts, that's as it should be, but why is it not so with the worldly people? These are just my personal thoughts.

I would think it is because they have not learned who the true God of their lives should be, and He alone is to be worshipped, so they cling to what they know and who they know.

It is the godly Ministers' duty to cause the people to understand; that the people belong to God and not to them; and they should not care so much for people that it becomes almost impossible to carry on in life without them, and that they should not follow the things that are temporary for they shall soon fade away, and then where are we?

Michael and Elvis are two other people that the world loved and followed like they did Miss Diana, Michael, Diana and Elvis were all doing things that caused their lives to end suddenly and tragically, yet they were the peoples idols, this is the world loving their own; this is another situation where this person is in the news for what seems like forever with much weeping and much travel Just to be in the same space where he is, even though he is dead.

Remember this?

Doing this same time period seven souls were brought back from Afghanistan in body bags, and we saw what was glimpses of one body coming off the air plane, and a little fanfare they being over- shadowed by a man that sang, popped and spin, and the world called him great, I ask the **Question When** will we as people become settled within ourselves when one dies, whether it is the President, a Celebrity, our mother or father, child or infant seeing that we all die at some point?

My answer.

Only when we have embraced the words of God and set them in our hearts; and allow them to soothe and comfort us in our Spirit.

What is your response to these thoughts and reactions?

Now there is man called Prince even some so called Christians are caught up in the hype concerning him.

Let the dead bury the dead, while the rest of the saints remember to live life while they are yet alive, in Jesus name

CHAPTER XI

Our surrender

What are some major causes for our great sufferings?

Denial might be number one. When a loved one is in a season or period of transition, and God is showing us that it is their time to depart: we should not continue to deny what is set before us; but we must begin to agree with God in His timing of the departure for this person; in other words, we must also do like the person that is in transition, that is, to do like Jesus, surrender our will into the hand of the Father for this event and for ourselves.

Anger is another emotion that we must deal with; we must address the cause for that anger.

Search yourself, and write about it, make this your own personal project in search of freedom: the devil don't care how he bind you.

Why are we in shock? That time of their suffering may have been more for us than for them, that we may have time to adjust ourselves to the forthcoming event, did we misunderstand the signs of death?

Suffering. Their suffering should help heal our suffering when we see their suffering has ceased. Can we let go and submit ourselves to what is, even in our pain?

Prayer

Please pray this prayer: Lord, cause us (me) to never be bereaved again, though I may be in a bereaved family. Lord release me from the shock, pain, suffering, sadness and anger which holds me in a fog, or in its grip, it is truly a place of un-realness, yet, it is so very real. I pray for total release from all of the emotion that continues to overwhelm me. Help me to surrender my will while I am in this suffering state unto your will in peace. In Jesus name.

Finally:

Our one and only great purpose:

This really is only the beginning of a great and important subject, if we were to search the scriptures, we would find that all of the people of the bible had one great purpose in their lives; even though they did many other things in life, including Judas Iscariot. Which betrayed Jesus.

Abraham:

Abraham's one and only great purpose in life was to bare the seed that would bless all nations of the world, him becoming the father of faith, and father of the nations of this world.

Sarah

Sarah's one and only great purpose for being in this life was to bring forth Isaac, the promised seed, bringing him forth in her old age showing us that God as EL (Almighty) Shaddai can restore life to the body at any stage in life. Genesis 21(KJV)

Joseph

Joseph, although he was cast into prison, and spent several years there doing other things,

His one and only great purpose for being in this life was to nourish up Israel, and to keep the nation of Israel alive.

Moses

Moses did many great things in his life, being raised up as a prince in the house of Pharaoh; learning leadership skills, and earning respect in the kingdom of men for forty years.

Moses spent another forty years learning new skills in the desert of Midian, leading or guiding sheep and goats like David. But, his one and only great purpose for this life was; to bring Gods' people out of Egypt from the house of bondage into the promised land of Canaan.

Saul-Paul

Paul although he was a persecutor of the saints, his one and only great purpose for being in this life was to bless the New Testament church, laying the foundation of the Gospel of Jesus, and to open up the Mysteries of God to the people through the revelation which he received, him writing several books of the New Testament.

Jesus

God came Himself as Jesus in the flesh, that is, as a man to save His people from their sins. Although He did many miracles and wonders in the land, His one and only great purpose for being in this life: was to take on Himself the sins of this world (all People) at Calvary. Him paying our sin debt, reconciling us back to the Father, defeating the work of Satan.

…To this end was I born, and for this cause came I into the world… St. John 18:37 (KJV)

These are only a few names mentioned, and their one and only great purpose in this life, Although we do many things passing through this life.

What is your one and only great purpose in this life?

_____

_____

_____

Are you functioning in it?

_____

_____

Yes

No

Why not?

_____

_____

_____

Do you know what your one great purpose is?

Yes

No

Why not?

_____

_____

_____

If not ask God.

If yes, thank God

Please don't allow the death of others to keep you in the graveyard to long, maybe these people have fulfilled their one and only great purpose in this life, and **is now called** back to the place of rest having their works to follow them. Revelation 14:13 (KJV)

Do you understand that we all have only one great purpose in life, after we have completed our assignment in life we must return back to our maker?

"Then shall the dust return to the earth as it was: and the spirit shall return unto God who gave it". Ecclesiastes 12:5 (KJV)

My Summary

This is my summary on the subject of death and dying, the warning of death, including the action of setting the house in order.

We have seen some great people of the bible be warned, die and be quietly put away, we have seen their worship, and also the results of their departure. We also have heard the time frame prescribed by God for the people's mourning.

It is my understanding that we are in error as to how we are dealing with this situation, also we may at a later time be called on the carpet **so to speak,** by God for not educating His people in such matters.

We have seen the sons of Aaron die by the hand of God for blatant disobedience. And we saw how Aaron, and his sons, and their Uncle Moses were to move on in their office as if all was well.

I acknowledge the fact that God has brought understanding to some through experience and revelation, but many others are yet to experience the suffering, and devastation of this grieving spirit for a lack of teaching.

God has given us teachers; and while we teach others let us teach ourselves.

Thou therefore which teachest another's, teachest not thyself? Romans 2:21 (KJV)

If we were too seriously search the scriptures we would find some interesting facts on how some of us have and could leave this life.

First it said, *and Enoch walked with God; and he was not; for God took him. Genesis 5:24 (KJV)*

This is meaning that God translated him without the natural death process, but no mention of any great mourning after they got over the initial shock that he was missing.

"And it came to pass, as they still went on, and talked, that, behold, there appeared a chariot of fire, and horses of fire, and parted them both asunder; and Elijah went up by a whirlwind into heaven", *2nd Kings 2:11 (KJV)* Representing our rapture.

But if this had been one of our parents, how long would it have taken us before we could have closed the book on this Chapter of our lives without having a body?

Some would live in this grief for a lifetime, because of a lack of biblical teaching on the subject of death and dying.

We did surely observe Moses response to the death of his nephews. Nadab and Abihu listed in the book of Leviticus 10:1(KJV) there was Moses himself in charge of the circumstances that surrounded the death of; not only his nephews, but his brother Aaron, also Moses you might say had to finalize the services of those whom he loved.

We heard Moses who not only set the house of God in order before his death, but he gave to us an example of the order for the future.

Then there was Jacob and Joseph, and there was David and Job

Aaron, Job, David, Martin and Moses taught us the most important lesson there is to learn; that is, how and when to worship God, and that we are to bless and curse not.

We especially took noticed of what Jesus Himself would do, and He being faithful to Him, and being who He is He worshiped also.

I count Jesus, Joshua, Abraham, David, Job, Moses, Aaron, Martin, John and Robert to be an elite group of people that we should observe and pattern our lives after, in the matters of death and dying, and in setting the house of God in order.

Setting the house of God in order

As leaders of the church we should set the house of God in order as they did in the Old Testament times, the house of God should not lay bare because the man of God died, or the Pastor stepped down from his duties, or was put out too pasture by his congregation for whatever reason.

The functioning of the church was never intended to be placed into the hands of the lay people such as the boards, deacons and trustees; because they were never ordain by God nor by men to lead and feed the flock of God, nor to watch for a man's soul. So it should be the order of the called shepherds of God to tend the house, and the flock of God.

There are too many men who have taken it upon themselves to become the head of the church, and to hold hostage the family of God by their positions and their ego's; all churches which operates without a Pastor is not, not I say! A complete church.

Any- **body** that do not have a head, has no life. Any person which believes any part of the **body** can function without their proper head may try leaving their heads at home, and see how well they fair without it in their day. There must be called ordained leadership in the house of God.

For the bible said: *For the husband is the head of the wife, even as **Christ is the head of the church; and He is the saviour of the body.** Ephesians 5:23(KJV)*

Paul writes to Titus and instructs him in the knowledge of who is to be ordained as Elders or Preachers to lead the flock, no mention of boards, deacons and trustees as Pastoral leadership in the Church of God. We may be able to trust the deacon to wait on the tables and to leave the women alone, and we may be able to trust the trustee to keep the money straight and the building in tact, but they are not called to intercede over the flock as the Pastors are called to do, so boards, deacons and trustees that control the churches; they are operating outside of their calling, and is sure to be severely judged by the Lord.

This one, or two man band control in this area should never be allowed: nor tolerated by the members of the church.

Bylaws should not govern the body of Christ: The Spirit of God, and the word which the Apostles gave to us should govern the body of Christ (the church) for it is His body.

Paul said this is the reason

…For this cause left I thee in Crete, that thou shouldest set in order things that are wanting, and ordain elders in every city, as I had appointed thee; Titus 1:4-5 (KJV)

I am sure many men shall be called on the carpet by God concerning His house, and His family.

Ezekiel said that we as Pastors and leaders have not done our part concerning His people; we have not caused the people to be healed.

The diseased have ye not strengthened, neither have ye healed that which was sick, neither have ye bound up that which was broken, neither have ye brought again that which was driven away, neither have ye sought that which was lost: but with force and with cruelty have you ruled them. Ezekiel 34:4 (KJV)

CHAPTER XII

Conclusion

I conclude that even the New Testament saints must learn what the Old Testament saints have learned, practiced and demonstrated to us through the scriptures, and we should be an excellent example to the next generation in how we should response to death and dying.

We should be able to carry on the assignment which has been assigned to our hands under any circumstances; we have seen the Old Testament principles; and the modern day man become one through John and Robert Kennedy and Martin Luther King Jr.

To our Ministers and lay people of God; it is imperative that we as Preachers, Pastors, Ministers and leaders of the church are found to be capable of making funeral arrangements, and officiating at funerals even when it is up close and personal without falling apart, especially when our own pain may be extreme.

We must continue to see this personal duty as part of our office in which we have been assigned.

If we are Preachers, we must continue on in our preaching, even to our family members and to ourselves in the mist of death and dying. This is not the time to step down from you calling.

If we are teachers, then we must continue on with our teaching, teaching ourselves and others in the mist of our bereavement by demonstration.

If we are Deacons, we must continue on in the waiting on of the tables toward others in our assigned duties with joy.

If we are pew members, surely we must continue on in our membership and fellowship with the saints without falling away; this is definitely not the time to quit nor become slack in our duties, and in our faithfulness to God and the Church.

We need the word and the fellowship of the saints more now than ever before, the enemy is looking for an open door to steal, kill and destroy us emotionally, mentally, physically, socially and spiritually.

I have also come to the understanding that death is not about age; sickness or tragedy, whether it is a sweet and quiet death or whether it is by violence; but death is only about escape after the completing of the assignment; when our assignment is complete we must depart this life. Most of all, we must have faith in our Lord Jesus Christ that He is working things out, as He did for the man in the book of Luke.

And, behold, there came a man named Jairus, and he was a ruler of the synagogue; and he fell down at Jesus' feet, and besought Him that He would come into his house:

For he had only one daughter, about twelve years of age, and she lay a dying. But as He went the people thronged Him Luke 8:41, 42 (KJV). While He yet spake, there cometh one from the ruler of the synagogue's house, saying to him, thy daughter is dead; trouble not the Master.

But when Jesus heard it, He answered him, saying, fear not; believe only, and she shall be made whole. Luke 8:49-55(KJV)

Let us continue on in the word which we have read, and have faith in the one who has called us to this mission it is He that will make us whole.

One might ask the question: how shall we survive the death of a loved one with dignity?

Answers

First: we take the initial thirty days which is allotted to us in Deuteronomy 34:8 (KJV) to reflect, and recall the good times of the past and the awkward moments as we weep.

Second: we begin to put all things into perspective weeping as we go, but letting go more and more every day, until that one which died is placed in the proper place in our hearts and minds.

Thirdly: we must move them further and further back into our memory, not as to forget them, but not to allow them to dominate the functioning's of our daily living.

We are much too afraid to let go of the dead in fear of betrayal or forgetting them, but the mind will work in our behalf if we would just follow the natural process in acceptance as children do. We unlike children hold on to the dead instead of releasing them to the calling of time. After thirty or more years without a death in our family. I had three close family members to die within two years, my step father at the age of 79 years, my sister who was 56 years young and my natural father at the age of 86 years. Yet I have my first tear to shed for either one of them, totally because of the word of God which I have heard, learned and believed.

It is because of the scriptures that I am in this place without the misery of grief in death. This is how we survive the reality of death without being caught up in the human experience of emotions; which causes us to repeat the emotion again and again.

The word of God is our permanent comfort without regret or longing for their return.

Here some might say, but you are a Christian and that's the way you think, and I'm not there yet, well you may be right, but the effects of death treats us all the same if we are not previously instructed in another way of dealing with grief.

God wants us all to be in the same place as His creation, and that is, in belief of His way of doing things. This is how we are spared many miseries of life.

When bereavement comes

When we are in bereavement let us embrace that which is written.

Revelation 14:13 (KJV) 1ˢᵗ Thessalonians 4: 13-18 (KJV) 1ˢᵗ Corinthians 15:51-57 (KJV)

These scriptures tells us that our dead in Christ are living, sleep, at rest, and happy.

Matthew 22:32 (KJV)… tell us that God is not the God of the dead, but of the living.

Disclaimer:

I do not claim to be proficient in this teaching on the subject of death and dying, however it is a starting point to open, and to invite others to join me in this effort to know, and understand the will of God for us in these horrific situations.

Printed in the United States
By Bookmasters